Triumphant in Tragedy

Finding Faith, Hope, and Courage in Your Darkest Hour

Kolbe Hill

Sermon To Book
www.sermontobook.com

Triumphant in Tragedy / Kolbe Hill
ISBN-13: 978-1-945793-23-3
ISBN-10: 1-945793-23-6

"When you are in the 'deep thick of trouble,' there is nothing you need more than truth ... and truth must have a messenger. Kolbe Hill is a master messenger of what he has seen and heard and experienced with God. He weaves a strong mix of humor, faith, and honesty in this book that will help you navigate your personal encounters with difficulty and tragedy. Read *Triumphant in Tragedy* ... then read it again. Let its truth soak through to your deepest panic, doubt, and fear and 'run it out of doors.' Kolbe Hill is alive today because God is not finished with him yet. I look forward to all Kolbe will pass on to his generation!"

—Pastor Nancy McCready – Executive Pastor at Christian City Fellowship in Sealy, Texas

"Pastor Kolbe is raw and real in every area of this most personal crisis. His pursuit to live and to rely upon God is an example to all who experience tragedy."

—Pastor Dennis Hill – Senior Pastor at The Remnant Church, La Grange, Texas

"Good stories are written every day, but great stories are the ones that are lived. You will be captivated by this story of fear, faith, and courage. Kolbe will take you on a journey that will help you understand more about God, encourage you to ask questions, and guide you to find those answers. We are blessed to know the author and now read his story. An excellent read for those that are facing any difficulties."

—Rob and Ginger Carmen – Victory World Missions

"Kolbe Hill is a believer who faced one of life's greatest challenges and found victory in Christ! I believe his victory can also be your victory. This incredible book, *Triumphant in Tragedy*, is a roadmap from darkness into light. I trust that no matter what you're going through, Kolbe's story, revelation, and wisdom will encourage you and increase your faith in Jesus and in His Word. This is a powerful book written by a wonderful Man of God!"

—Phillip Baker – Phillip Baker Ministries

To my wife. I still can't believe I'm kissing Rachel Hill.

CONTENTS

In Our Darkest Hour

When tragedy and trials strike close to home, do you prepare for surrender—or gear up for battle?

For my part, I was ready to fight.

I began writing this book shortly after receiving the news of a tragedy in my life. I had faith that God wanted victory in my life and would walk me through the battle.

It wasn't until a few years passed and the dust settled, however, that I realized I had made one crucial mistake in fighting the good fight of faith: I had applied all the principles, but I was missing the person of Jesus.

I had received my miracle and had been healed from an incurable cancer, and should have been excited about it, but instead I was tired and depressed. Why? At first I thought I was crazy, but now I can see the answer is simple: I had been fighting with His tools, but without Him! Though the following pages are full of helpful tools to assist you when faced with tragedy, only you can choose to go to Him.

In the Gospel of Matthew, Jesus encouraged believers, "Come to me, all you who are weary and burdened, and I will give you rest" (Matthew 11:28 NIV). The first thing God wants believers to do when faced with a trying situation is come to Him. He is your source. He is your supply. Scripture even goes so far to say that apart from Him, the believer can do nothing (John 15:5), but you can do all things through Him who gives you strength (Philippians 4:13).

I was tired because I had used His tools while fighting in my own strength. His tools can only be properly used when He is using them through His people. That can only happen by coming to Him.

I avoided God when first faced with this trial, because I was, in fact, mad at Him. I was angry because I was so young and I thought the situation wasn't fair. I had bought the lie that modern Christianity often teaches: when you give your heart to Jesus, you won't have a care in the world.

But the Bible doesn't teach that. Instead, God's Word encourages followers of Jesus to "Cast all your anxiety on him because he cares for you" (1 Peter 5:7 NIV). Jesus never promised everything in life would be hunky dory. He did promise that when the storms of life arise, He will provide shelter from the storm.

Perhaps you picked up this book because you are experiencing one of the most difficult, dark times of your life. Be encouraged—you are in the company of the Bible's finest. The greatest men and women of God in Scripture were not immune to difficulty. God included their stories in the Bible so they could instruct and assure believers.

Consider Proverbs 3:5–6:

Trust in the LORD with all your heart and lean not on your own understanding; in all your ways submit to him, and he will make your paths straight. **— Proverbs 3:5–6 (NIV)**

Sometimes God's ways make no sense. Tragedies certainly don't. But they are not terrible—in fact, in God's eyes, they are often good. Are you ready to look your trial, tragedy, or difficulty square in the face and "lean not on your own understanding," but trust His?

Equipped with Faith

The intent of this book is to be a tool that will help those suffering from any form of tragedy—to help them stand in faith through life's darkest hours. It is in this season people find themselves drowning in fear, doubt, and sorrow, flailing and grasping for anything to keep them from going under.

I know this feeling well, and my prayer is that the following pages will provide handles—practical principles you can grab onto and apply. I know from personal experience that these principles can bring stability in a time when it seems like everything is uncertain.

Thus, the workbook section that follows each main chapter of the book includes reflective questions and an application-oriented action statement to help you begin relating these practical principles to the trials you face.

My encouragement as you begin to apply these biblical principles to your specific situation is not to forget who is most important in any season: Jesus. Your relationship with Him is the very thing you need above all else to be victorious.

CHAPTER ONE

An Unexpected Tragedy

It was a Sunday afternoon in early February 2010, right after an incredible church service. The message and fellowship had been powerful.

As was our custom after a long morning at church, we went home, fed the kids, and put them down for a nap. After everyone's belly was full and the kids were sound asleep, it was time for my wife and me to take a nap of our own.

I slept on the couch for about an hour and woke up with a horrible crick in my neck. As I put my hand on my neck to rub it, I felt something unusual. There were strange lumps under my ear and continuing down my neck to my collarbone. I was extremely alarmed, but since it was Sunday and all of our small-town doctors were closed, there was nothing I could do.

As soon as the doctor opened the next day, I secured an appointment to check out my newfound lumps. Of course, the enemy was bombarding my mind with the worst. My doctor immediately diagnosed me with mono, and the blood test to follow would confirm his hunch—disaster diverted.

In the months to follow, all of the lymph nodes went away in my neck except for one directly above my collarbone. The doctor seemed concerned, and eventually his concern landed me at a specialist.

This doctor was not concerned by the swollen node at all, however, and believed it to be a scarred node from the mono. I was satisfied with this verdict and continued on with my life.

But as the next few months went by, these unusual symptoms continued, which led my doctor to send me to another specialist. This guy was less help than the first guy, and he too sent me away with a clean bill of health.

At this point I decided to take matters into my own hands. I knew that at the age of twenty-eight, I should not be struggling with all of these health issues. I prayed about what I should do.

At the time, I was extremely overweight, so I didn't have to wait for an answer to my prayers—I just used my God-given common sense. I knew I needed to lose weight and regain the health God had so ordained for me. Under the direction of some friends in our church, I started a diet and was on my way.

Over the course of about four months I lost fifty pounds and was feeling healthy. All my strange symptoms went away, except for the lymph node above my collarbone.

A New and Improved Me

I was excited about my new lifestyle and felt better than ever. I was fairly confident that the persistent lymph node in my neck was nothing more than what the specialist had said it was—a scarred lymph node. Still, in the back of my mind the question "What if?" lingered.

That "what if" became one step closer to reality while my family and I were on vacation in Destin, Florida. It was a trip to which we had looked forward for months.

But on the twelve-hour drive to a stress-free week with my family, my arm began to ache. It wasn't much at first, so I thought maybe it was some discomfort from the drive. However, by the time we arrived in Destin, my left arm had doubled in size and had turned a nasty shade of blue. The pain was so intense I had trouble carrying the luggage and our kids to the room.

After a shower that night, I went to put on deodorant and discovered painful and swollen lymph nodes in my armpit. Shortly afterward, my groin began to ache and the lymph nodes began to swell there as well. My entire body was freaking out—and I was terrified!

The many lies the enemy had been whispering in the back of my mind were now on the forefront of my every thought. I attempted to have fun and be normal for my family's sake, but no matter how hard I tried, the stress from the situation won out.

Needless to say, the vacation was an absolute disaster. All I could do the entire trip was look at my wife and little girls and wonder what the future had in store for them. What in the heck was wrong with me? Would I be around for them? Would I be able to provide for them?

I wanted the answers to these questions, so as soon as we returned home, I was on my way to another specialist. However, this time I had strict orders from my doctor to biopsy the lymph node.

Life-Changing News

It was November 29, 2010, at 8:49 a.m. when my cell phone rang. I knew from the number it was the doctor with the results from my biopsy. I answered the phone in faith to hear the good report for which we had been praying.

I could tell immediately from the doctor's tone that I needed to brace myself for bad news. The calm, cold words that came out of his mouth would change my life forever: "Kolbe, you have cancer."

My entire body went numb and I could not respond. After all, I was twenty-nine-years old and in the best health of my entire life. How could I have cancer?

The results from the biopsy were only preliminary. They did not know exactly what kind of cancer it was, but it didn't matter. *I had cancer.* I hung up the phone and went to find my wife and gave her the news.

Neither one of us knew what to do except to hold each other and cry. All I could think about were my one- and four-year-old daughters. The enemy wasted no time in filling my mind with fear, doubt, and unbelief.

I joke now when I tell my story by saying my wife and I "did it" everywhere after that phone call. We did it in the bed. We did it in my office. We did it in the shower. We did it on the couch. We did it in the car. We even did it in the doctor's office—all of the places we *wept* together. We were totally broken and lost.

The days after the initial news are a blur to me. They were filled with tests and doctors and more tests. I will never forget standing outside of one doctor's office with the giant word 'Oncologist' on the wall and thinking, "What in the hell [excuse my language] am I doing here? I don't belong here! Someone pinch me, because surely I am about to wake up from this nightmare."

Finally, I was diagnosed with stage four mesothelioma, which is a cancer in the lining of the lungs. This type of cancer is most commonly caused by years of asbestos exposure and generally found in people over the age of seventy. I met neither of these criteria. The doctors had no clue as to how I could have developed this disease.

To make it even more of a mystery, not only did I have the cancer in the lining of my lung, but also in the lining of my abdominal cavity, and it had spread throughout my entire lymphatic system as well. My body was completely riddled with cancer. For someone my age to have a disease like this was so rare that the doctors could not even give me a percentage on how rare it was.

The diagnosis from the pathology report was so difficult for the doctors to believe that they decided to do a minor surgery and place a small camera in my abdomen to see exactly what was going on.

The day of the procedure was January 18, which was my wife's twenty-ninth birthday. Because the doctors had a hard time believing their own diagnosis, we had hope that maybe, just maybe, this was all just one big mistake. Rachel wanted nothing more for her birthday than to have that doctor come into the waiting room after the procedure and tell her they were wrong and this had just been a mix-up.

They wheeled me back to the operating room, and as they put the gas mask over my mouth, I prayed that I would wake up to a miracle. I believed with all my heart that God was going to heal me completely.

As I awoke from the procedure, the first person I saw was Rachel. I could tell she had been crying, and I wondered if they were tears of joy or of sorrow.

As my vision cleared, she looked into my eyes and I could see nothing but heartache and pain. At that moment, before a word was said, I knew my prayer for a miracle had not been answered—at least not the way I wanted it to be answered. We didn't say anything to each other; we just cried.

The doctor came in shortly after I woke up, and in his hand was the proof that I was most certainly going to die, barring divine intervention. He handed us pictures of the inside of my abdomen, completely covered with tumors. It broke my heart that the only gifts I had to give my wife on her birthday were disappointment and despair.

After receiving my diagnosis and prognosis, the next step was treatment. The doctors gave me only one treatment option, and that was chemo. Radiation was too dangerous for certain areas of my cancer, and there was no surgery option.

I was told my disease was terminal. The chemo could possibly control it for a while, but ultimately doctors could not cure the disease. Death was inevitable, and I had around six months to live. My perfect world—a job that I loved and a family that was too good to be true— was slipping away and I couldn't seem to stop it. I left the doctor that day with no hope from the medical world.

Being a pastor, I had helped many people through various tragedies in their lives, and had even experienced a few bumps of my own. But this was definitely the most difficult thing I had ever undergone. I felt emotions I had never experienced and came to know fear like I had never known it before.

Until this point I thought I had a pretty good handle on faith, and was sure that I was ready to handle anything the enemy could throw at me. I quickly learned I was not fully prepared for what was ahead. This was the greatest trial I would ever face.

I tell my story not to try to impress anybody or to try to gain anyone's sympathy, but to earn my readers' trust. The pages ahead were birthed in the midst of tragedy.

I realize there are people who have gone through trials far greater than mine. I am reminded of the young family in our congregation who lost their eight-month-old daughter to a brain tumor. For the majority of their baby's life, they never knew her outside of a hospital room hooked up to tubes and wires.

As I am writing this, another family in our congregation has just received news concerning their eight-year-old grandson that his treatment for bone cancer was not effective, and he does not have much longer to live.

There are people all over the world who are dealing with circumstances they never thought they would have to face. If you are reading this book, it is likely because you are facing a tragedy of your own. The bottom line is that whatever you are facing, whether great or small, it matters greatly to God.

More Than Many Sparrows

At one point in His ministry, Jesus forewarned His disciples of trials they would face. They would be arrested, flogged, betrayed, and hated because of Him (Matthew 24:9). However, Jesus comforted them, telling them not to be afraid:

> *Are not two sparrows sold for a penny? Yet not one of them will fall to the ground outside your Father's care. And even the very hairs of your head are all numbered. So don't be afraid; you are worth more than many sparrows.* — **Matthew 10:29–31 (NIV)**

God knows what each of His children are going through, and He cares. Back in Genesis 28:15, God reminded the Israelites, "I am with you and will watch over you wherever you go" (NIV). In Deuteronomy 31:6, He promised He would "never leave you nor forsake you" (NIV). And Jesus, before leaving this earth, comforted His disciples saying, "Surely I am with you always" (Matthew 28:20 NIV). You are worth more than many sparrows.

If what you are experiencing is big to you, it is big to God and He cares. His presence will be with you through every circumstance—good or bad. I'm confident that though the difficulty you may be facing is dark, weighty, and probably terrifying, God has a good plan and purpose for you in it.

My experience with cancer played out over what seemed like an eternity. That experience has given me a new appreciation for this precious gift called life. It is out of this tragedy that God birthed a passion in me for those who are hurting. I, too, know what it is to be afraid, to doubt, to be angry, and to question God. However, through all of these struggles, I learned what it means to be triumphant in tragedy.

WORKBOOK

Chapter 1 Questions

Question: Look up and read Psalm 61:2. What circumstance in your life feels too big for you? How can you seek and accept God's help in this situation?

_____

_____

_____

_____

_____

_____

_____

_____

_____

_____

_____

Question: With what fears are you contending in your life now? How, exactly, can you hand these fears over to God?

_____

_____

_____

_____

_____

_____

_____

_____

_____

_____

_____

_____

_____

Action: When an experience feels too big for you, and fear and despair threaten to overwhelm you, trust that God cares about your situation—and has a plan for you!

Chapter 1 Notes

CHAPTER TWO

Don't Wait Until It's Too Late

Ever since I was a child, one of my passions in life has been hunting. Growing up, I was surrounded by some of the most prime hunting opportunities in the world. Texas is home to the beautiful and elusive white-tailed deer, and I have spent countless hours in the deer stand hunting and observing these amazing creatures.

One of the reasons I enjoy hunting these animals is because of the challenge. These deer are smart! Their sense of smell and incredible eyesight make them exceptionally difficult prey. After all the time I've spent watching these deer, I have no doubt God has instilled in them an instinct to survive. They have spotted me thirty feet up in a tree and ducked under my arrows traveling over 260 feet per second. They were created to survive.

On the other hand, encountering a white-tailed deer on one of Texas's dark country roads is a dramatically different story. The phrase "deer in the headlights" can't fully be appreciated until a person experiences it.

These smart, agile, and built-to-survive animals completely change when caught in the blinding beams of a vehicle's headlights. It is like their God-given instinct to survive is ripped from them and they freeze with fear. Their ability to run and jump is disabled by the shock of being out of their element. Paralyzed and distressed, they don't move. These deer are left with only the hope that the vehicle will pass them, leaving them unharmed.

The sad part is, more often than not, the story ends differently. Because the deer chooses to close its eyes and wait for the nightmare to pass, it winds up as what we Texans call "road kill."

Did the deer's life have to end that way? No! If the deer would have used its God-given ability to survive, rather than responding in fear, the animal may have escaped death. Unfortunately, most of the time the "deer in the headlights" waits until it is too late to make a move.

Caught in the Devil's Headlights

People are not a whole lot different from the white-tailed deer. When in their element, they are amazing—relying on God-given abilities not only to survive, but also to thrive. Then a tragedy strikes. No one anticipates or plans for catastrophes, illness, or sudden death. Most people certainly don't know how to handle it when it happens. No, tragedy shows up like it does for the deer facing a car at night. One minute everything is great, but the next minute, the world seems to be falling apart.

Tragedy comes in all shapes and sizes. Whether it is the loss of a loved one, the loss of a job, a bad doctor's report, or an unexpected divorce, the enemy loves nothing more than to take that opportunity to rattle your faith—like the deer in the headlights.

On November 29, 2010, at 8:48 a.m., my life was fine. I was sitting at my desk and working like I always do. I was in my element, cruising through life. But at 8:49, I found myself in the middle of a dark road, stuck in the beam of the devil's headlights. I was frozen in fear and in complete shock.

That feeling of dread is one I will never forget. I knew what I needed to do, but I was frozen. It was like my ability to think clearly and make rational decisions had completely left me. I wanted to deny the news I had just received and wait for everything to pass. I felt alone, afraid, and defeated.

My wife could tell I was struggling, so she suggested that I reach out to a ministry friend of ours for help and advice. But I was stuck. I could not move toward asking for help. Despite her pleas, I refused to call our friend. I was numb, and my will to fight was gone.

I did not realize it at the time, but I was in a critical stage of my difficult journey. I was in the middle of the road and could not move. However, a person facing tragedy cannot afford to stand still. Even though pressing on may feel near impossible, it's critical to fight back against the enemy's voice. If not, there is a high possibility of winding up on the "front bumper" of the enemy's attack.

It is so tempting when in the midst of difficulty to sit back and hope everything will turn out okay, but that is not what God intends for believers. He calls us to rise up and fight!

God promises in His Word He "works for the good of those who love him, who have been called according to his purpose" (Romans 8:28 NIV), especially when they experience tragedy. Followers of Christ don't have to wait until a trial or difficulty passes before experiencing victory.

Frozen in Fear

There I sat, however, denying the problem as if it would one day evaporate. But frozen in my funk, I remembered a sermon my pastor had preached about the children of Israel.

The nation of Israel was hemmed in between Pharaoh's army and the Red Sea. As Moses described the Israelites' predicament, "The Egyptians—all Pharaoh's horses and chariots, horsemen and troops—pursued the Israelites and overtook them as they camped by the sea near Pi Hahiroth, opposite Baal Zephon" (Exodus 14:9 NIV).

God's people were in trouble! The biggest and baddest army in the known world was after them, and there was no clear escape. Unfortunately, how the Israelites responded in this tragic situation is the way so many Christians respond when faced with difficulty.

Moses continued, recounting what happened next:

As Pharaoh approached, the Israelites looked up, and there were the Egyptians, marching after them. They were

*terrified and cried out to the LORD. They said to Moses,
"Was it because there were no graves in Egypt that you
brought us to the desert to die? What have you done to us
by bringing us out of Egypt? Didn't we say to you in Egypt,
'Leave us alone; let us serve the Egyptians'? It would have
been better for us to serve the Egyptians than to die in the
desert!"* — **Exodus 14:10–12 (NIV)**

The Israelites—who had just been miraculously released from four hundred years of Egyptian
oppression—looked at their situation and complained,
questioned, and blamed. They were doing a lot of things
in that moment, but they weren't moving. They were
stuck.

The Israelites' bitterness and unbelief weren't helping
to solve the problem. In the crosshairs of Pharaoh and his
army, they froze with fear. They had given up before
God had a chance to deliver them. This is how defeated
people respond.

So many people find themselves stuck in the midst of
difficulty! Stuck people do the same things—they complain, question, and blame.

If you were standing in the middle of the road with an
eighteen-wheeler careening toward you going eighty
miles per hour, I bet you wouldn't complain, question, or
blame. No, you would get the heck out of the way! You
would run, jump, and do anything else you could think
of to remove yourself from the path of destruction. However, when tragedy strikes, many people sink into a funk
and accept defeat.

Be Quiet and Move On

Recall the Israelites' sour attitude when trapped between the Egyptian army and the Red Sea. Moses responded to their complaints with assurance from God:

> *Do not be afraid. Stand firm and you will see the deliverance the LORD will bring you today. The Egyptians you see today you will never see again. The LORD will fight for you; you need only to be still. Then the LORD said to Moses, "Why are you crying out to me? Tell the Israelites to move on." — Exodus 14:13–15 (NIV)*

That phrase "be still" does not mean to stand still—it means to be quiet. Here the Israelites were watching their lives flash before their eyes. They were complaining, questioning, and blaming. They were defeated before the actual fight had begun. God grew tired of their faithless chatter, and basically told them to "shut up and move!" in Exodus 14:15.

They were not getting anything accomplished by standing still. This tragedy was not going to pass by. If the Israelites continued whining without moving, they would have become Egyptian road kill. It took God saying to "shut up and move" for the Israelites to take that first step of faith toward the Red Sea.

In the end, God parted the water and the Israelites crossed safely to the other side. The entire Egyptian army drowned in the middle of the Red Sea (Exodus 14:21–28). The Israelites' amazing story of redemption illustrates how imperative it is to trust God and step out in faith in the middle of a difficult situation. He will be faithful to carry those who do!

Triumph in the Midst of Tragedy

But the story doesn't end there. The next chapter in Exodus describes the Israelites dancing and singing songs of victory to the Lord.

The Israelites knew how to be triumphant *after* tragedy, but they did not know how to be triumphant *in* tragedy. Anyone can sing a song of praise when they are on the other side of a trial, but it takes a courageous man or woman of God to sing and dance in the midst of their trial. How easy it is to rejoice in song about what already happened, but it takes an incredible amount of faith to sing a song about what is yet going to happen. Though it may seem crazy, this is the kind of faith God desires.

I will never forget sitting back in my chair and thinking about the lessons I had learned from this story. Would I let this truth fall to the wayside and remain stuck, or would I shut up and move? Would I put my head in the sand and hope to be triumphant after the tragedy—and risk being pounded by what was ahead— or would I decide to rejoice in the Lord regardless of whether I was healed from cancer or not? Would I press on and be triumphant in tragedy?

I could not get this story out of my head, so I decided to make a move. I chose to heed my wife's advice and called our friend. In my defeated state, I complained, I questioned, and I blamed. My friend quietly listened on the other end.

When I was finally finished, I expected him to cry and feel sorry for me. I expected him to be sensitive to my situation. I expected him to be like me and not have any answers, but that was not the case.

His words literally shook me—they were not kind and sympathetic, but harsh and demanding. I felt like I was talking to my high school football coach, not a ministry friend. Instead of being sympathetic, he chewed my butt out. I couldn't believe it!

I will never forget our conversation. He said, "Kolbe, you can lay here and be defeated, or you can get up and grab a hold of the victory that is available right now." It was in that moment that I had a choice: I could either lie down and die, or rise up and make a move toward my victory.

At the time, I was almost a little offended at my friend's insensitivity towards my situation, but now I thank God for it. I am so glad he did not stand in the middle of that dark road with me, but yelled loudly enough for me to come back to my senses and move to a safer place. His words to me were like God's to the children of Israel: "Shut up and move!"

Embrace the Reward Ahead

My prayer is that this chapter would be those words to you. Though they may seem harsh and insensitive, if received, they are life-saving. I know how difficult it can be to rejoice, praise God, and embrace triumph in the middle of tragedy. But I also know how necessary it is.

The apostle Paul exhorted believers in the Philippian church:

> *Brothers and sisters, I do not consider myself yet to have taken hold of it. But one thing I do: Forgetting what is behind and straining toward what is ahead, I press on toward the goal to win the prize for which God has called me heavenward in Christ Jesus.* — **Philippians 3:13–14 (NIV)**

There is a reward ahead, and it is this prize God wants you to focus on—not your current circumstance.

I know how serious and weighty the beginning of a trial is. There is nothing you can do about the past, and often you can't change your current situation. But there is something you can do about the future.

Every tragedy has purpose—but don't wait until you understand it before experiencing victory. In those first hours, days, and months of a trial, reach down deep in your faith and do not accept defeat, but move toward victory. Shut up and move!

WORKBOOK

Chapter 2 Questions

Question: In what situation or aspect of your life are you stuck right now? How are you responding, or attempting to become unstuck?

_____

_____

_____

_____

_____

_____

_____

_____

_____

_____

_____

Question: How does the Word of God want you to respond when you're stuck in a difficult situation? What is

one specific, biblical response you can adopt toward
your difficulty?

_____

_____

_____

_____

_____

_____

_____

_____

_____

_____

_____

Action: When you are stuck in your difficulty, frozen in
fear, don't wallow in defeat! Instead, be quiet, move on,
and embrace the reward ahead.

Chapter 2 Notes

_____

_____

_____

_____

_____

_____

_____

_____

_____

_____

_____

_____

_____

_____

_____

_____

_____

_____

_____

_____

_____

_____

CHAPTER THREE

Empowered by the Word

"There is nothing we can do for you."

I will never forget sitting in the room with my wife and the oncologist. He was giving me the prognosis of my diagnosis, and though he might not have spoken those exact words, they were the gist of his message. I was basically told to go home, hug my kids, and get my affairs in order.

Completely devastated, I left that day feeling totally helpless. Those words "there is nothing we can do" kept playing over and over in my mind, and for a moment I was convinced they might be right. I felt helpless.

The Facade of Control

Helplessness is a common response for someone facing a tragedy. It is a feeling that results from believing that what is done is done, and nothing can fix it. Most people are accustomed to being in control in their lives.

They control what time they wake up, what they eat, and what they wear. If something unexpected comes up, they are usually able to adjust and compensate for those surprises.

But a true tragedy is more than a surprise—it is something that forces a person from any element of control and leaves them feeling completely powerless.

I have always loved music, so it's not uncommon for me to associate a song with a situation—just about everything reminds me of one song or another. It may be something someone says or something I see that brings certain lyrics to mind.

After the doctor left the room, I slumped in my chair in front of the table, overwhelmed with this feeling of doom. It was in that moment that an old Darlene Zschech song, "My Hope," began to rise up inside of me. The lyrics to that song pounded in my spirit: "My hope is in the Name of the Lord, where my help comes from!"[1]

I couldn't have sung another line from the rest of the song, but that was all I needed. I knew God was speaking to me, letting me know that I was *not* helpless, and He was my help. I was *not* completely powerless! All the way home, I sang the line from that song.

After a while, I grew curious. How exactly was God going to help me? What was going to be His amazing plan to dig me out of this seemingly unfixable situation? The feeling of helplessness had left me, and I was feeling empowered, but I wasn't quite sure with what yet. The doctors had told me there was nothing to be done, but I knew in my heart there was something I could do. I was on a mission to find out what.

That night at our weekly church prayer service, I stood up to give the congregation the update from my doctor. As I shared the grim news with my friends, people began to come forward to pray and lay hands on me.

It was right then that God answered the question I had been asking Him on the way home. It wasn't prayer, laying on of hands, or anointing oil that would help me—it was the Word of God. I wasn't helpless! There was something I *could* do, and it was right in front of me. It was *in* me!

I was so excited about the plan God had given me that I told everyone to sit back down. I had already been prayed for, hands had been laid on me, and I had been anointed with oil. Now it was time to be empowered by the Word.

I grabbed the microphone and began to quote every Scripture I knew. I didn't care if it had anything to do with healing or not. All I knew was that the Word was my answer. The doctor had his word, and now it was time for God's Word to take center stage.

I quoted Scripture from Genesis to Revelation, and everywhere in between. When I couldn't think of any more Scripture to quote, I opened a Bible and started reading verses out loud. I knew I wasn't helpless anymore.

I don't know what you are facing right now in your life, but whatever it is, you are not helpless. You have the Word of God.

God's Word Sustains

I will never forget the first day I was in Bible school at Texas Bible Institute in Columbus, Texas. Pastor Tommy Burchfield stood up and quoted more Scripture than I had ever heard in my life. He loved the Word and taught me to love it, too. Over the two years I spent there, I can't tell you how many times I heard Pastor Tommy say, "Put the Word of God in you when you don't need it so it will be there when you do need it."

Now, at the time, I was an all-knowing and all-powerful Bible school student who didn't completely agree with Pastor Tommy's philosophy. I didn't know quite what he meant by "putting God's Word in you when you don't need it." In my arrogant, nineteen-year-old Bible school student's mind, I believed I was more spiritual than Pastor Tommy because I *always* needed the Word of God.

Despite my arrogance, I did what Pastor Tommy taught me. I learned how to fill my mind and heart with God's Word for the two years I was at Bible school, and I found I continued to hunger for and meditate on His Word after I graduated.

It wasn't until I experienced personal tragedy that I more fully understood what Pastor Tommy had taught me. Scripture I had placed in my heart years before welled up inside me to empower me in the depths of my despair.

I am so thankful now that I put the Word of God in me when I didn't need it—because I had a deep well from which to draw when I *did* need it. It is paramount that believers store up the Word of God for difficult times they cannot yet see. The Word of God is so important that Jesus used it to refute Satan saying, "It is written: 'Man does not live on bread alone, but on every word that comes from the mouth of God'" (Matthew 4:4 NIV).

God's Word is eternal, and it is as essential for believers as food. It is the only thing that will sustain you during difficulties. Though things in this life come and go, the prophet Isaiah wrote, "The grass withers and the flowers fall, but the word of our God endures forever" (Isaiah 40:8 NIV).

Time to Brush the Dust Off

Though it contains the words of life, many believers do not study the Scriptures, much less know them by heart—though it is common for Christians to own several copies of the Bible. However, understanding some basic truths about God's Word may help instill a new respect for this divinely inspired book.

The Bible is one of God's greatest miracles. It is a collection of sixty-six books that consist of 1,189 chapters. Those 1,189 chapters are made up of 31,102 verses.[2] Of those 31,102 verses, there are nearly 800,000 words. The Bible was penned by forty men over a period of approximately fifteen hundred years, in three different languages, from three different continents. Despite the fact that most of its authors never knew nor collaborated with each other, the Bible contains no historical errors or contradictions.

The Bible contains some three thousand promises. There are approximately 2,500 prophecies in the Bible, 2,000 of which have already been fulfilled without error. The other five hundred refer to future events that have not unfolded yet. The fact that this book has stood the test of time over twenty centuries is nothing short of miraculous. The psalmist wrote, "The LORD's word is flawless," (Psalm 18:30 NIV) and that it "is perfect, refreshing the soul" (Psalm 19:7 NIV). Because of this, God's Word calls for utmost respect and reverence.

God's Word is alive and active (Hebrews 4:12), God-breathed (2 Timothy 3:16), and blesses those who hear it and obey it (Luke 11:28). It gives understanding (Psalm 119:130), and God says those who put His instruction into practice are wise (Matthew 7:24).

These are just a few verses revealing the benefits of studying Scripture and putting God's Word in your heart. To allow dust to collect on the very breath of God is an insult to the divine plan of the Creator himself. It is a privilege to freely possess the single greatest thing on earth—the Bible—and therefore, it is paramount that believers esteem it more highly than anything else.

Job understood the importance of God's Word—elevating it above everything else in life. He wrote, "Neither have I gone back from the commandment of his lips; I have esteemed the words of his mouth more than my necessary food" (Job 23:12 KJV). The Word of God is supposed to take precedence over all things.

I am so grateful that in the midst of a horrible time I chose not to let my emotions, the doctor's opinions, or my physical condition determine my future. Instead, I allowed the eternal Word of God to shape what was ahead.

Second to Last

Back when I was in seventh grade, I wanted to participate in every sport. I was heartbroken when football season came to a close in the fall, but I was excited about the upcoming spring sports. It was going to be track season.

I had never run track before so I wasn't sure what event I would be the best at. In my mind, I was probably going to be the best at all of them. I imagined myself leaping over hurdles and crossing the finish line in first place. I dreamed of pole vaulting through the air and long jumping into that really cool sandbox.

The first day of track practice came, but much to my surprise, the coach didn't put me on the hurdles, the mile relay, or pole vault. No, the coach took one look at me and sent me to shot put.

You see I was never what you would call thin—but I had heart. I wasn't afraid to *try* anything, but the reality was, I wasn't good at everything. In seventh grade I was just as wide as I was tall, and I would have snapped the pole vault pole like a toothpick!

None of those realities mattered to me, however. I wanted to run like the wind and fly through the air with everyone cheering for me as I crossed the finish line in first place. I did not, however, want to throw some stupid lead ball with all the other fat kids.

I was a little offended at the coach's decision, but gave in and learned how to throw the shot put anyway. It was about half way through track season and I was growing weary with the lead ball, but I refused to quit.

Finally, my moment of glory came.

It was a hot and muggy Saturday morning track meet, and I and all my "big boned" friends had finished throwing the shot put. We were in the bleachers watching the different running events. It came time for our team to run the one-hundred-yard dash, but one of our runners had gotten sick. More than one runner was needed to compete in the race.

Most of the other kids were tired from running other races, but I was still fresh! After all, the only thing I had done was chunk a shot put a few times.

I was convinced that I was the man that could take our team to the top—all I had to do was convince the coach. I pitched the idea to him. Though he wasn't quite on board, my peers came to my rescue. They began to join in with me and tell the coach that I should run the race. They rallied behind me and left the coach with no choice but to let me run.

Finally, I wasn't the only one who believed I could run track, because my friends believed it, too! My wife—who was at that track meet—tells me now that they only wanted me to run so they could make fun of me, but I choose to believe they wanted me to run because they knew I could win.

My feet stepped onto the track with confidence. I wasn't wearing track shoes, but with skills like mine, I didn't need them. Intimidating my competition with my stare, I prepared to run.

Bang! The starting gun went off and I took off like a cheetah chasing a gazelle.

I don't remember a whole lot for the next one hundred yards—I was running so fast, everything was a blur. All I could hear were my fans screaming my name and my heart pounding. Starting to tire, I began to slow down. I could feel the pressure of another runner coming from behind, so I kicked it into another gear.

I crossed the finish line and the entire seventh grade track team came cheering to congratulate me. It hit me— that was the farthest I had ever run without stopping! I was struggling to breathe and felt like I was going to have a heart attack, but I didn't care.

After all the commotion settled down, I found out that I had not won the race. I didn't come in second. I had come in second to last.

To this very day, I thank God for the kid who was slower than me. Even though I didn't come in first, I didn't come in last—I wasn't the fastest, but I wasn't the slowest!

God's Word Always Comes First

People often treat God's Word like a fat kid running the one-hundred-yard dash. They cheer for it, think it's fun, and occasionally let it entertain them. But it always comes in second-to-last place.

God's Word should never come in second to last—it should always hold first place.

Consider what the Bible says in Hebrews 11:3: "Through faith we understand that the worlds were framed by the word of God, so that things which are seen were not made of things which do appear" (KJV). The Word of God existed before anything visible to the human eye.

Not only did it exist eternally, before anything else came to be, but it also did the creating. John 1:1 in The Message version says, "The word was first," and John 1:1–3 says:

> *In the beginning was the Word, and the Word was with God, and the Word was God. He was with God in the beginning. Through him all things were made; without him nothing was made that has been made.* *(NIV)*

That is why greater value must be put on the Word and what it says: because the Word existed before all things, it is sovereign authority.

Before I became sick—the Word. Before you were hurt—the Word. Before you were lied to—the Word. Before you were offended—the Word.

When the Word takes first place in a person's life, it empowers them. Their emotions, other people's opinions, their circumstances, and their physical conditions all come after the Word. Thus, those things must bow to the authority of the Word.

Who Told You That?

Some believers need to get back to the beginning. After I was diagnosed with cancer, I longed for a day in the future when I was cancer free. Before I could move forward to that day, I discovered I had to go back to the beginning. The only way to overcome past and present difficulty is to remember the Word of God always has the *first* word over our lives.

In the beginning, God created the heavens, the earth, and every living creature in it. Then He created His masterpiece: man and woman (Genesis 1). In Genesis 3, Adam and Eve were deceived by the serpent in the Garden of Eden, and chose to eat of what God had forbidden. As a result, they hid from God in shame and attempted to cover their naked bodies (Genesis 3:8).

God was not unaware of what had happened. The Bible says the Lord "called to the man, 'Where are you?' He answered, 'I heard you in the garden, and I was afraid because I was naked; so I hid.' And he said, 'Who told you that you were naked? Have you eaten from the tree that I commanded you not to eat from?'" (Genesis 3:9–11 NIV).

I love that God asked Adam, "Who told you that you were naked?" God didn't—but Adam knew. That understanding came from the devil. That word came *after* God's word about Adam. Adam listened to the devil's voice and it destroyed him. God's Word empowers us, while the word that comes afterward wants to destroy us.

Right now, I believe God is asking believers the same question He asked Adam: "Who told you that?" Who told you that you were fat? Who told you that you were worthless? Who told you that you were stupid? Who told you that you couldn't do it? Who told you that you could never recover?

God didn't. Those words came *after* what God said from the beginning of time about His people, and thus, those words do not have the greater authority. Remember and be empowered by what God has said from the beginning, and see His Word come to pass in your life.

The doctors told me I was going to die, but I went back to the beginning in Psalm 118:17 which says, "I shall not die, but live, and declare the works of the Lord" (KJV). That is the word I chose to believe and elevate to first place. That is the word that empowered me in the midst of my tragedy.

The Bible addresses every need in any given situation—there are truths in the Bible that can help everyone. Those who are sick might be encouraged to read the Gospels which overflow with stories of how Jesus healed people. Those who are downcast will find comfort and be uplifted through the Psalms. When faced with persecution, the Bible provides encouragement to fight the battle through Old Testament stories of victory. And when a person needs direction or wisdom for what to do, the Proverbs abound with truth of God's perfect wisdom.

Test Every Word

Some thoughts come from God, and some from the enemy. It is important that believers not listen to every thought, for some deceive. To do this, believers should test every thought by running it through the 2 Corinthians 10:5 test—especially before allowing it to take residence in their heart. Paul said:

> *We demolish arguments and every pretension that sets itself up against the knowledge of God, and we take captive every thought to make it obedient to Christ.* — *2 Corinthians 10:5 (NIV)*

Ask yourself if the word you are receiving lines up with what God's Word says about you or the situation. If it doesn't, cast it out.

People deal with tragedy in many different, human ways—which will never bring peace. Followers of Jesus must deal with it according to the Word of God. Difficulty is not a time to close the Bible, but rather to open it up and seek God's comfort, peace, and direction. When you're experiencing trials and tribulations, it is time to place God's Word far above all else. He will deliver you from fear, doubt, worry, and anger.

Giving the Word first place empowers those who trust His ability to move forward and see victory.

Chapter 3 Questions

Question: What is your personal relationship with God's Word? How much time have you spent reading, studying, and learning God's Word? How has the Word helped you through difficult moments in the past?

_____

_____

_____

_____

_____

_____

_____

_____

_____

_____

_____

Question: How, specifically, can you begin to deepen your relationship with the Bible so Scripture is at your ready disposal when needed most?

_____

_____

_____

_____

_____

_____

_____

_____

_____

_____

_____

Action: Learn and memorize Scripture as a regular habit so God's Word remains near your heart, especially at times of great difficulty. Trust that the Bible is the first word in any situation, and look to the Word to empower you to move forward into victory!

Chapter 3 Notes

CHAPTER FOUR

Empowering Those Around You

When you're faced with tragic adversity, only one thing has the power to carry you through, into undiminished life and genuine victory.

It's God's Word—and you must cling tightly to it.

However, doing so doesn't mean the tragedy will evaporate and life will return to normal. Most of the time, it doesn't.

One of the hardest things to do when experiencing any tragic difficulty is learning how to come to grips with the uncertainty and downright scariness. One of the things I found out when I was diagnosed is that I was not the only one who was struggling with properly dealing with my situation. Everyone around me was also struggling with what to do, what to say, and how to act. Just as much as it was a shock to me, it was a shock to my family and friends.

Unintentional Avoidance

Most people have no clue how to handle others who are going through tragedies—they certainly didn't know how to handle being around me. I had been on the other side of this coin many times, but it was strange being on the flip side.

You know what I'm talking about. Any time someone is going through a tough situation, it is hard being around him or her. You feel sorry for them, but you don't really know what to say—it can be awkward. Because of this, most people do what is easiest and avoid the person.

I had shied away from many people in my day, but now I was the one being avoided. I can remember being in the grocery store. The people who would normally come and say "hi" were ducking down the baby food aisle, and I knew for a fact they didn't have a baby! People didn't know what to say, so they didn't say anything.

There were a few people who wound up being in a situation where they had to speak to me, and they all did the same thing. They tilted their head a little to the side and sighed all while looking at me with sad puppy dog eyes. It was like they were saying, "I'm so sorry. It must be really hard knowing that you are going to die soon."

Then they would start petting—literally petting—me like I was their family dog moments before it was going to be euthanized. Some would even start crying and hugging me like it was going to be the last time we would see each other. I would always think to myself, "Why are *they* crying? No one has told *them* they are going to die!"

These were supposed to be the people who would stand strong while I was weak. I was supposed to be leaning on *their* faith while mine was wavering. But no! They were already planning my funeral. I couldn't be too mad at any of them, because I had made the same mistake many times as well.

The reality is, people are not going to know how to respond to your situation. This is especially true for those who are closest to you. Family and close friends who love you may be overwhelmed by their emotions accompanying the tragedy. While you are dealing with fear, anger, and sorrow, they likely are as well. Their emotions may cloud their better judgment, and they may wind up unintentionally hurting you more than helping.

I waited and waited for someone to step up and take responsibility for my situation. I was looking for that special person who could magically understand what I was going through and help me through it, but that person never came. People kept avoiding, crying, and petting me.

I was tired of hiding. I was worn out from the awkwardness. I was saddened by people's lack of faith. Being a pastor, it wasn't just a few people I had to deal with, but a whole congregation. I had been empowered by God's Word and was feeling so much better. My faith was strong! But the people around me weren't on the same page.

Empower Others with the Word

I was sitting in my office one afternoon and reading a list of confessions I had written concerning my health and future. You see, I knew God's Word was my answer. I knew what I was believing God for in my life. I recited those Scriptures every day. I was declaring the Word of the Lord over my life!

About that time, my phone rang. It was a good friend of mine. I shared with him the Scriptures I had been declaring. Then I started whining to him about how people were responding to my situation.

His response to me was life-changing. He said, "Kolbe, instead of just expecting people to know how to handle your situation, teach them how you want them to handle it. You have been empowered by the Word, now empower them."

It was so true! Instead of hoping everyone would figure out how to handle the situation, I should have been empowering those with what I had been empowered with.

Let's face it. Whether the issue is a health battle like mine or a death in the family—regardless of what it is—most people won't know how to handle it. Because of that, people's natural tendency will be to withdraw, but the truth is, the person going through the tragedy desperately needs others. No tragedy can be overcome alone!

In times like these, it is crucial to have a support team. A boxer or an MMA fighter never heads to the ring alone. The fighter always has an entourage of support. From the person carrying a banner when the fighter enters the arena to the guy holding the spit bucket, no significant battle is won alone.

Who is on your team? Instead of avoiding and being avoided, instead of being frustrated, instead of dreading those awkward conversations, instead of being afraid that some will say the wrong thing or ask the wrong question, empower those around you with what *you* have been empowered with. Release the vision and direction of your faith and encourage those around you to join in. You will find those same people whose conversation you used to dread are now people to whom you look forward to talking because they refresh your faith.

Don't waste any more time. Begin to empower others and experience the unexpected blessings that will result.

Unity Strengthened in Tragedy

Throughout the Bible, God reveals His heart for unity. It is a blessing that often blossoms during difficult times. King David understood how beautiful unity can be. He wrote, "How good and pleasant it is when God's people live together in unity!" (Psalm 133:1 NIV).

God loves unity. Discovering that God's plan is for His people to be surrounded by those of like faith is utterly liberating.

The devil, on the other hand, hates unity. John wrote in his Gospel the enemy's goal is to "steal and kill and destroy," (John 10:10 NIV). Satan is the author of division and longs for God's people to feel isolated and sorry for themselves when going through trials.

I am reminded of a story in 1 King 18. A great prophet of God, Elijah, was proving God's greatness by slaying 450 prophets of Baal. Elijah seemed to be invincible until he received word that Queen Jezebel wanted him dead. The Bible reveals that Elijah grew afraid and ran for his life. First Kings 19 describes Elijah alone in a cave, defeated and depressed. Then Elijah heard God's voice:

"What are you doing here, Elijah?"

He replied, "I have been very zealous for the LORD God Almighty. The Israelites have rejected your covenant, torn down your altars, and put your prophets to death with the sword. I am the only one left, and now they are trying to kill me too." — 1 Kings 19:13–14 (NIV)

This sounds like so many people when they're going through a difficulty. They begin to make statements like, "No one understands what I'm going through," and, "I'm the only one who feels this way." That is a lie. Those kinds of thoughts don't promote unity, but instead move a person toward isolation and depression. Elijah believed these lies, and they wound up costing him his ministry.

The Lord continued, telling Elijah there were seven thousand strong men and women of God still out there! (1 Kings 19:18) That was Elijah's team! But instead of relying on his team's strength during a difficult time, he retreated to the cave of defeat. Don't make the same mistake. God has hand-picked some great men and women of God to come along side you in the midst of difficulty.

Imagine if instead of running from his team of seven thousand, Elijah had empowered them with the same power he had received. There would have been revival in the kingdom like never before. If Elijah had been empowered to call down fire from heaven and destroy 450 prophets of Baal, what could have happened if Elijah had empowered seven thousand others to do the same?

Are you starting to see why it is so important to embrace and include those God has placed on this journey with you and ultimately to empower them? Solomon understood this when he wrote, "Two are better than one, because they have a good return for their labor" (Ecclesiastes 4:9 NIV). Together is better!

The importance of unity is highlighted in the story of the tower of Babel. It takes place after the flood. The Bible says people were beginning to re-establish themselves in the earth.

Now the whole world had one language and a common speech. As people moved eastward, they found a plain in Shinar and settled there.

They said to each other, "Come, let's make bricks and bake them thoroughly." They used brick instead of stone, and tar for mortar. Then they said, "Come, let us build ourselves a city, with a tower that reaches to the heavens, so that we may make a name for ourselves; otherwise we will be scattered over the face of the whole earth."

But the LORD came down to see the city and the tower that the people were building. The LORD said, "If as one people speaking the same language they have begun to do this, then nothing they plan to do will be impossible for them."
— Genesis 11:1–6 (NIV)

What an incredible story and beautiful illustration of the power of unity! It says that they all spoke the same language—they were all on the same page. This was so huge it got God's attention. God went so far as to say that if they continued in this type of unity, nothing would be impossible for them.

Now to be clear, these were ungodly people trying to reach an ungodly goal. Soon, the Lord confused their language (Genesis 11:7–9). God knew all He had to do was disrupt their unified minds and hearts and they would not be able to accomplish their goal.

But just because this story doesn't lead to a happy ending for the people of Shinar doesn't mean there is not a powerful principle we can learn from their story. If nothing was impossible for a bunch of ungodly people trying to reach an ungodly goal, how much more possible will it be for a bunch of godly people to reach a godly goal?

Unity is the key. Surrounding yourself with people who are on the same page and speak the same language is critical when difficulties arise. They will help keep your focus on God and His Word and will understand your needs in a way that goes beyond the physical.

Teams Tap into the Power of Agreement

When you have a team of brothers and sisters in Christ who are operating from the same word God has given you concerning your situation, unity is the natural outcome and Jesus shows up. Matthew recorded Jesus' own words regarding the mysterious blessing that comes from working together in Christ:

> *Again, truly I tell you that if two of you on earth agree about anything they ask for, it will be done for them by my Father in heaven. For where two or three gather together in my name, there am I with them."* — **Matthew 18:19–20 (NIV)**

Empowering your team with agreement is a powerful biblical principal—and the result is God's presence among you. I don't know about you, but I want Jesus in my midst!

Before I empowered those around me, they were agreeing with all the wrong stuff. They didn't mean to. It just came naturally. As soon as everyone found out what type of cancer I had been diagnosed with, they went and looked it up on the Internet. If you do a Google search of mesothelioma, the results are pretty grim. That is why so many sad puppy dog looks and sympathy pets came my way.

Without realizing it, people were agreeing with the prognosis of my diagnosis. They were agreeing with fear and defeat instead of faith and victory. That is why it was so crucial for me to get them agreeing with the right stuff! The world's prognosis was certain death, but the Lord's prognosis was long life. I was believing in faith for long life, and it was my responsibility to help those God had placed on my team to do the same.

My decision to do this put into motion the biblical law of agreement. My friends and family were not just agreeing with *me*, they were agreeing with *God*! I was no longer alone asking God for a mighty deliverance, but hundreds of people, whom I had enlisted to agree with God concerning my life, stood with me.

Now the power of God could be released at a greater capacity according to His promise—when two agree on earth about anything they ask, "it will be done for them by my Father in heaven" (Matthew 18:19 NIV). Whatever difficulty you are facing, surround yourself with a faithful few who will seek God in agreement. According to Matthew 18:19, it will be done.

Teams Tap into the Power of Vision

When those who surround you are empowered to be unified and in agreement with what God says about your situation, their perspective begins to change. They begin to get a vision, not of where you *are*, but of where you are *going*.

True vision sees beyond the difficulty in front of you. As my team began to declare God's Word over my life, people began to see past cancer. People quit planning my funeral, and they started planning my future. We quit talking about where I was and started talking about where I was going!

I remember playing pee-wee football when I was a kid. I was definitely a better football player than track star! I loved football with every fiber of my being. It was the only time I was allowed to hurt people on purpose, and I loved it.

At eight years old, I was in a football league that was classified by weight instead of age, so that the individuals playing against each other were relatively close to the same size. Now, if you knew me at eight years old, you would know this did not work out to my advantage. We weighed in before each game to make sure we were under the weight limit. I was on the ninety-five-pound max team. But I will never forget showing up to a game one morning and weighing in at ninety-nine pounds. I was not allowed to participate in the game and was forced to move up to the next weight class.

This was a whole new ball game. I now went up against kids way older than me. I went from being the biggest and the baddest to one of the smallest and youngest.

The coach put me in at left tackle. I did my best, but the other team had a linebacker that was eating my lunch. Every time I hit him, I would bounce off. It seemed like the harder I tried, the worse it hurt.

My dad called me over to the sideline and I began to cry in frustration. I explained to my dad that no matter how hard I hit the guy, I ricocheted off him. My dad then gave me what I considered at the time the worst advice ever. He said, "Stop hitting him."

What? That was my job! If I didn't hit him, he would sack the quarter back. My eight-year-old suspicions that my dad knew absolutely nothing were confirmed.

After I finished telling my dad what an idiot he was for giving such horrible football advice, I let him finish talking. He continued: "Don't hit *him*, hit five yards past him." The problem was, I had been hitting the linebacker instead of hitting *beyond* the linebacker. When I hit him and stopped, I bounced right off. My dad was advising me to hit *through* him—not to aim for him, but to aim past him. I took his advice, and the next play I aimed five yards past the linebacker. To my amazement, I creamed the guy. The problem wasn't the big bad linebacker, but where I was aiming.

The problem isn't the big bad difficulty you are facing. Rather, the problem is where you are aiming. Vision is important because it enables you to see *past* the problem to the victory. Instead of slamming into the problem and stopping short, vision moves through the problem and reaches the goal.

When you and your team begin to operate in unity and agreement, it changes your perspective, giving you vision to see past the tragedy to the victory that waits ahead.

A Letter and an Invitation

Gathering people in unity and agreement and giving them vision was a crucial part for me in making it through tragedy. One way I accomplished this was through a letter I sent to my family and church congregation. This letter was a tool to assist me in empowering them to know how to handle the situation I was going through:

Hello Church!

I wanted to take a moment and thank everyone for their prayers and support in this time of testing for Rachel and me. I am so grateful for the family God has given to help me through this time. What an honor it is to help pastor this incredible congregation. I believe that our best days are ahead! It has been so exciting to see all the new faces and families coming and growing in the truth. Just as much as Rachel and I are receiving all the prayers and faith for us, please know that we are daily standing in faith with you and your family. We are all in the faith, so we know that we are all in the battle. But what a privilege it is to hold forth the precious gospel to a lost world—no matter the cost!

I was encouraged the other day with the story of the "Tower of Babel." How amazing it is to see the power of unity in this story. The Bible says the people all spoke one language and had one voice and nothing was impossible for them. Wow! In this story, ungodly people were trying to reach an ungodly goal and nothing could stop them as long as they spoke the same language. If this principle worked for an ungodly people, how much more will it work for the people of God? My point is this: my health is under attack, but Rachel and I have chosen to travel the road of faith. We are believing and speaking God's Word on a daily basis. We believe what God's Word says about me is more of a reality than what any doctor or report says about me. What if we were all believing and speaking the same thing—speaking the same language? Nothing would be impossible to us!

I have shared this with you all to ask you to join your faith with ours in a very specific way. I have listed below some of the things that Rachel and I are declaring by faith on a daily basis. We have all been praying generally for my healing, but the below declarations are specific things the Lord has given me concerning my life, health, and future. Please join with Rachel and me in daily declaring these things. As we all speak the same language, I believe nothing will be impossible to us. Jesus has done everything He is going to do; now let's access that power by declaring His Word!

With the letter, I provided a list of scriptures that Rachel and I were declaring out loud on a daily basis:

1. Kolbe was healed by the stripes of Jesus. (Isaiah 53:5; Psalm 30:2, 107:20)

2. Kolbe's best days are ahead. (Ecclesiastes 7:8; Job 8:7)

3. Kolbe's future is bright; it is full of hope, prosperity, and success. (Jeremiah 29:11)

4. Sickness and disease will not consume Kolbe's hands, but his hands will consume sickness and disease. (Mark 16:17–18)

5. Kolbe is full of faith. (Mark 11:23; Hebrews 10:38–39, 11:1)

6. Sickness and disease *cannot* take residence in Kolbe's body because his body is the temple of the Holy Ghost. (1 Corinthians 3:16, 6:19)

7. Kolbe does not have a spirit of fear but of power, love, and a sound mind. (Psalm 112:7; 2 Timothy 1:7)

8. Kolbe is being overwhelmed by the peace of God. (Isaiah 26:3; Philippians 4:7)

9. Kolbe will preach the Gospel well into his nineties. (Psalms 20:4, 23:6, 91:16)

10. Kolbe will give his daughters away to better men than himself. (Proverbs 22:6)

11. The anointing on Kolbe's life is increasing. (Psalm 92:10)

12. Kolbe daily walks in victory. (Romans 8:31, 8:37; 1 Corinthians 15:57; 2 Corinthians 2:14; 1 John 4:4)

13. Kolbe walks in divine wisdom. (Proverbs 2:6; James 1:5)

14. 2011 will be Kolbe's healthiest year ever and there is nothing the devil can do about it. (3 John 2)

15. Jesus is Lord over Kolbe Hill!

The results were amazing. People no longer hid from me, and the awkward conversations ended. The absolute best part was that people quit petting me! I was no longer alone in a dark cave of depression, but was surrounded by an awesome team of warriors.

The bottom line is, most people around you won't know how to respond properly to your situation. Whether through a letter, a gathering at your home, an announcement from the pulpit, individual phone calls, or an email, assist others in agreeing with God, not with the world, about your situation.

Though this may be difficult in the moment, it is critical that you rise up and empower those God has placed around you—with the same Word with which He has empowered you.

WORKBOOK

Chapter 4 Questions

Question: How have others responded to a difficult circumstance or trial in which you found (or find) yourself? What vision of your situation did their reactions reflect or project?

_____

_____

_____

_____

_____

_____

_____

_____

_____

_____

_____

Question: With what specific vision of your situation did you need others to agree in faith and unity during your difficulty? What are some specific steps you could have taken (or could take) to help other people get on the same page, in faith, about your situation?

_____

_____

_____

_____

_____

_____

_____

_____

_____

_____

Action: When people don't know how to respond to your tragedy or trial, empower them with the Word! Tap into the power of unity and agreement in faith, which enables you to have a clearer vision for what lies ahead.

Chapter 4 Notes

CHAPTER FIVE

An Atmosphere of Hope

Many people, especially followers of Christ, claim to believe in miracles.

Yet how many people can say they've experienced a life-saving miracle first-hand?

In the months following my diagnosis, I traveled to MD Anderson in the Houston medical center countless times. They tested my blood, took x-rays, and performed CT scans to make sure the cancer hadn't spread.

These visits were hard: I had to take off work, spend days away from my children, and pay for hotel rooms and all the other expenses that came with doctor visits. But despite the difficulty, I knew these appointments were the only way to confirm the miracle the Lord was working in my body. Each visit, I learned the cancer had not spread—and even more miraculously, it was going away.

Heaven's Medicine for the Hurting

There was one particular visit I remember well. My wife had always gone with me before, but this time, because of our kids' schedules, she wasn't able to do so. This wound up being a good thing because the office overscheduled people that day. I ended up being shuttled to another location.

If you have never been to MD Anderson or a similar place, it is truly unbelievable—it is its own city, built by disease. The first few times I was there, I was overwhelmed not just because of its size, but also by the number of people with cancer. It helped me understand what David meant when he wrote, "Yea, though I walk through the valley of the shadow of death..." (Psalm 23:4a KJV).

Everywhere I looked the shadow of death lingered. It was a sad and depressing place that—to me—was seemingly void of any kind of hope.

After much confusion and being sent back and forth across the entire campus a few times, I finally arrived at the right spot. I was prepped for my exam and placed in a room full of other patients—some very sick people. The atmosphere was oppressive and there wasn't much conversation. The few patients who were talking shared their stories of doom. It seemed as if they were comparing stories to see whose disease was worse!

I was still waiting to be called back, so I decided to join in on the conversation. As I got to know the other folks, I discovered most were new patients, some diagnosed the week prior. Most were gripped with fear and uncertainty about the outcome of their situation. I could see they all had one thing in common: hopelessness. They were prisoners to fear, prisoners to a diagnosis, and prisoners to the professional opinion of man.

I couldn't handle much more negative talk, so I began sharing my story with the patients. Everyone listened quietly as I told them there was hope in Jesus. I could feel the atmosphere changing and could see their countenance transform. All of a sudden, several people were laughing and joking, and others started talking about their families and jobs. In just a matter of minutes, everything shifted. Why?

It was hope! It was right then that the Holy Ghost spoke to me and said, "Hope is heaven's medicine for the hurting."

Hope! Amidst tragedy, the enemy wastes no time in robbing people of their hope. But without it, there is no healing; there is no future. Every tragedy, no matter what kind, has one thing in common: pain. The medicine heaven provides to heal that pain is hope. Whatever burden you are currently facing, do not lose hope.

The apostle Paul wrote a letter to the Ephesian church, encouraging its people to remember what life was like before trusting Jesus:

> *Remember that at that time you were separate from Christ, excluded from citizenship in Israel and foreigners to the covenants of the promise, without hope and without God in the world.* — *Ephesians 2:12 (NIV)*

There was a time when you, too, didn't have Christ in your life, when you didn't have any hope. But if you have believed in Jesus as your Lord and Savior, you are not alone and you are not without hope. Just as Jesus gave me hope for my situation and shifted my vision, He will give you hope, too.

As you read this chapter, I am praying the same prayer Paul prayed in Roman 15:13: "May the God of hope fill you with all joy and peace as you trust in him, so that you may overflow with hope by the power of the Holy Spirit" (NIV).

God is more than a nice idea. He is the sovereign King of the universe and the giver of good gifts. He is the "God of hope." He wants His people to *have* hope, but also for that hope to overflow to others. Heaven's medicine is available to you, but also to everyone around you.

Stop right now and boldly declare you are overflowing with hope. When you do, your vision will shift away from your disease, your financial situation, or your loss, and toward the One who offers something greater: peace, comfort, rest, healing—and *hope*.

I watched this happen in my own life as I continued to agree with God's promises for me in His Word. At every doctor visit, I asked the doctors for good news. As the fluid in my lungs went away and my lymph nodes stopped swelling, I said things to my doctor like, "That's good, right?"

They consistently responded with something along the lines of, "Yes, but we don't want to get your hopes up only to be disappointed." They called it "false hope."

It used to really upset me that they never offered any kind of hope, but now I realize they were doing their jobs and what they had been trained to do—keep themselves out of a lawsuit.

Hope of the Glory of God

I was wrong—I was looking for hope in my doctors. To the world, and to my doctors, hope is nothing more than wishful thinking. It has no reality and is nothing more than fantasy. It is a wish upon a star that people don't take too seriously, because they know it will only lead to disappointment.

This is not biblical hope, which is more than wishful thinking. It is a confident expectation. Paul described this kind of hope as generated out of difficulty:

> *And we boast in the hope of the glory of God. Not only so, but we also glory in our sufferings, because we know that suffering produces perseverance; perseverance, character; and character, hope. And hope does not put us to shame, because God's love has been poured out into our hearts through the Holy Spirit, who has been given to us.* **— Romans 5:2–5 (NIV)**

Suffering may be present, but it produces perseverance, character, and ultimately hope that never disappoints. Biblical hope confidently expects to come out of a trial alive and kicking. Those with this kind of hope know beyond a shadow of a doubt they will not be let down.

The possibility of disappointment is why so many people are afraid of hope. The big "what if" holds them back. "What if I trust God and I don't get healed?"

To avoid disappointment, people choose not to hope at all. This action contradicts Romans 5:5, which declares biblical hope will never disappoint, because God has given us the Holy Spirit. This is where faith comes in. Either you believe God to be faithful to His Word, or you don't—and your choice will make all the difference. The writer of Hebrews said, "Faith is confidence in what we hope for and assurance about what we do not see" (Hebrews 11:1 NIV). Though you cannot know everything in the future, or what will happen next week for that matter, you can hope in the One who promises He will never leave you or forsake you (Hebrews 13:5; see also Deuteronomy 31:8; Joshua 1:9; Matthew 28:20).

Perhaps you are reading this and thinking, "But what if it doesn't work?" Stop! Followers of Jesus are believers and not doubters. Turn the "What if?" around and start asking, "What if it *does* work! What if I *do* get healed? What if my marriage *is* restored? What if I *can* rebuild? What if I *can* move on?" This attitude will create an expectation that will give birth to hope and will ultimately lead to victory.

God's people have been held captive by fear, doubt, and unbelief for too long. Now is the time to claim the restoration promised through the prophet Zechariah, who declared: "Return to your fortress, you prisoners of hope; even now I announce that I will restore twice as much to you" (Zechariah 9:12 NIV). You are a prisoner no longer, and God is ready to restore to you what was lost.

Consider the great men and women of God mentioned in Hebrews 11—people of faith who looked ahead to what they could not see and trusted God regardless of the outcome. As Hebrews 11:39 says, "These were all commended for their faith, yet none of them received what had been promised" (NIV). They hoped and believed what God had promised was true until their dying breath. Though they held fast to the vision God set in front of them, they were never privileged to see it come to pass.

In spite of this, they clung to hope. This is the kind of hope on which you need to agree with God while experiencing tragedy.

While reading Hebrews 11:39, the Holy Ghost spoke to me and said, "It is better to die believing than to live in doubt." With this mindset, losing is impossible. Hope is the confident expectation that God is going to come through on your behalf.

Tragedy may have had its hour in your life. Its voice has been heard, and its effects have been felt.

But now it's God's turn. Now is God's hour in your life. His voice will be heard, and the effect of His power will be felt. This is where the believer's hope is to rest.

Confidence in the Right Team

A man approached a little league baseball game one afternoon. He asked the boy in the dugout what the score was. The boy responded, "Eighteen to nothing—we're behind."

"Boy," said the spectator, "I'll bet you're discouraged."

"Why should I be discouraged?" replied the little boy. "We haven't even gotten up to bat yet!"[3]

What a picture of hope—when the believer's confidence isn't in the opposing team, but in their own team.

Last time I checked, you and I play for team Jesus. The Bible affirms that with Jesus, victory is possible: "If God be for us, who can be against us?" (Romans 8:31 KJV). Though the enemy may try to dissuade you and cause you to fear and doubt, remember whose team you are on. God is on your side, and nothing can stop His victory.

I identify with that little boy in his baseball game. As a kid I loved baseball. I played it every chance I got. There were plenty of times when my team was down and out, in the bottom of the ninth inning—it was a terrible feeling. Everyone's head would hang low and the dugout would grow quiet. Sometimes I would find myself wishing the game would end so the pain of losing would stop.

It was usually around that time one of my teammates or myself would do the unthinkable. One of us would stand up and face the rest of the team. They would reach up slowly and remove their cap, turn it backward, and flip the bill up. The whole team knew what this meant.

It was the rally cap, the signal that even though we were losing, the game was not over. We weren't giving up! There were still three outs to go and anything was possible in those three outs. One by one we would all put on our rally caps and morale would return to the dugout. Our attitudes flipped from packing our stuff to screaming and rattling the dugout fence.

More often than not, someone would get a hit, we would gain momentum, and we would win the game. Why? Because one person had hope.

Hope can change an entire atmosphere. You may feel like your situation is over, but place it in an atmosphere of hope and you can win. Embrace the psalmist's words when you doubt God's promises:

You, LORD, are a shield around me, my glory, the One who lifts my head high. I call out to the LORD, and he answers me from his holy mountain. I lie down and sleep; I wake again, because the LORD sustains me. I will not fear though tens of thousands assail me on every side. — *Psalm 3:3–6 (NIV)*

The X-Factor

One of my favorite parables Jesus taught is the parable of the sower. It is an amazing parable with a ton of spiritual application. I have probably preached more messages on this parable than any other passage of Scripture.

In the parable, a farmer goes out to plant his seed in the field, and the seed lands on different types of soil. There are different results for each type of soil, but to keep it in the context of hope, I want to focus on the end of the parable. Mark described what happened when the seed fell on good soil: "It came up, grew and produced a crop, some multiplying thirty, some sixty, some a hundred times" (Mark 4:8 NIV).

This story has always fascinated me. How can the same seed with the same soil produce different results? The one who sows the seed—the farmer—is God, who is good (Mark 4:14). The seed is His Word, which is also good. The ground is good, because the story says it's good. But somehow the harvest winds up different.

This doesn't seem to make sense. Let's look at it as we would a math problem. It would be like saying 3+3+3=30, or 3+3+3=60, and 3+3+3=100. I am no math scholar, but I am smart enough to know that doesn't add up. I did take math courses long enough to know that if you are adding the same numbers and getting a different product, there must be a missing factor. So in this parable, the math problem must look like this: $3+3+3+x=30$, $3+3+3+x=60$, and $3+3+3+x=100$.

Now we are getting somewhere! There is an x factor—a variable. We know there is a good farmer, good seed, and good soil. Now all we have to do is figure out the variable.

I live in a small town, so it is not uncommon to be at the local hardware store or feed store and find a bunch of old farmers hanging out. In all my years of being around farmers and listening to them talk, I have heard a lot of chatter about their harvest. Whether it was a record-breaking harvest or it was the worst harvest they have seen in fifty years, they love to talk about it.

The years when they remember the harvest being especially bad, their reason was always the same. It was never because they were a bad farmer. And I've never heard them blame the bad harvest on the seed. To this very day, I have never heard a farmer blame a bad harvest on the soil, either. *Never.*

It always comes down to the one thing that farmers have been blaming for as long as farmers have been farming: the weather. Great harvests happen when it rains and the sun shines at the right times. The x factor is the weather. The variable is a product of the atmosphere and the climate.

That is why in the parable of the sower, there were different harvests. Some thirtyfold, some sixtyfold, and some one-hundredfold. Each harvest was impacted by a different atmosphere, which determines outcome.

Circle back, now, to hope. Hope is the atmosphere needed for tragic situations. God (the farmer) is good, and God's Word (the seed) is good. For those who have received Christ into their lives, the ground (the soil) is good. Now it is up to believers to place their circumstance in the right atmosphere to receive a miracle, and that atmosphere is hope.

Whatever your situation is—a broken marriage, a prodigal child, a terminal illness— whatever it may be, when placed in an atmosphere of hope, everything changes. Hope transforms vision from impossible to possible.

Placing your situation in the climate of doubt, negativity, and unbelief will breed darkness and doom. You will surely miss out on God's outcome for your situation. But Scripture says "the LORD delights in those who fear him, who put their hope in his unfailing love" (Psalm 147:11 NIV).

When I walked into that hospital waiting room, surrounded by sick people and began to speak life and hope into their life, the atmosphere changed. Hope truly is heaven's medicine for the hurting—it brings about heaven's harvest. Allow God's Holy Spirit to pour hope into your heart—you will not be disappointed, and you will sense God's delight.

WORKBOOK

Chapter 5 Questions

Question: Where are you placing your hope amidst your current difficulties? Where should your hope be, exactly?

_____

_____

_____

_____

_____

_____

_____

_____

_____

_____

_____

Question: What fears or uncertainties threaten to diminish your hope in your difficult situation? How exactly can you fortify your hope to banish all doubt?

_____

_____

_____

_____

_____

_____

_____

_____

_____

_____

_____

_____

_____

Action: When facing trials, don't forget the crucial *x* factor—hope! Maintain your hope in the glory of God, who gave us His Spirit. Instead of fearing disappointment, have confident expectation in God's plan for you. Give no quarter to doubt!

Chapter 5 Notes

_____

_____

_____

_____

_____

_____

_____

_____

_____

_____

_____

_____

_____

_____

_____

_____

_____

_____

_____

_____

_____

_____

_____

CHAPTER SIX

Asking the Right Questions

Dr. Peter C. Wilcox, who specializes in helping people deepen their relationship with God, has written a book entitled *There Are No Right Answers to Wrong Questions.*[4] Have you ever found yourself asking the wrong question of your circumstances?

I have learned the importance of focusing on the right questions, and the folly of pursuing the wrong ones, in the midst of tragedy as well as everyday life.

By contrast, many people have claimed, "There are no dumb questions." Well, that is frankly ridiculous. People ask me dumb questions every day. Whoever first argued there are no dumb questions undoubtedly was arguing in self-defense, because there *are* dumb questions. There are wrong questions. There are questions that don't lead to anything productive.

The Best Glass of Tea

Let me illustrate this idea of poor questions with an interaction I had with my wife not too long ago. My family loves tea. I love tea. My wife Rachel loves tea. We live in Texas, so we drink a lot of tea! We like our iced tea un-sweetened, maybe with a little flavor and lemon. There is nothing better than a cold glass of tea on a hot day.

I have memories of my mother making sun tea. She would take that big clear pitcher with a yellow top and a sun painted on the side of it and put it out on our back patio to brew in the hot Texas sun. I love my mother's tea. I don't know if it is the taste, the way the ice gets soft, or how the condensation gathers on the outside of the glasses I have been drinking from since I was a kid. I don't know what it is—her tea is just good.

One day, Rachel was getting ready to make a pitcher of tea. We had been married for over ten years at this point, and in my mind I had been patient with her tea-making skills. But this particular day I thought maybe I could challenge her to step up her tea-making game.

Now don't get me wrong—her tea was good, but it wasn't *great*. It was up until this point in my life I believed the idiot who said there were no dumb questions. So I asked her: "Do you think you could get with my mom and let her show you how she makes tea?"

Wrong. Question.

She responded with silence, which in my house is far worse than yelling. She calmly made the tea, took out a cup, and poured herself a glass. I didn't know what to do, but I was thirsty so I went to pour myself a glass as well. Rachel, in a calm and kind voice said, "Don't drink that tea. If you want tea, you should go to your mom's and get some."

I knew I had messed up big time with that dumb question. For the next few months, I was not allowed to drink my wife's tea. The truth is I didn't deserve it. It was during those months that I came to love and appreciate her tea.

God has changed my heart, and I now love my wife's tea more than any other tea in the whole world. As a matter of fact, when we are at my mom's house now, I don't even drink tea—I drink water. Rachel, if you're reading this, your tea is the best!

This story proves the fact that indeed, there are dumb questions. Some questions lead people down a path that they don't want to travel.

While in the midst of a tragedy, there is a question that everyone wants to ask, but it is the wrong question: Why? Why did this happen to me? Why did this happen to my family? Unfortunately, this should never be the go-to question when faced with difficulty.

King Solomon addressed this in Ecclesiastes. He said, "Do not say, '*Why* were the old days better than these?' For it is not wise to ask such questions" (Ecclesiastes 7:10 NIV). It's not wise for you, either.

When I was first diagnosed with cancer, *why* was the only question I could ask. It became my favorite word. Why me? Why so young? Why should my wife have to go through this? Why should my kids have to grow up without a father? *Why?*

The Question That Goes Nowhere

Solomon said in Ecclesiastes 7:10 it is not wise to ask *why,* though it always seems to be the central theme of tragedy. When something unplanned happens or when a situation doesn't make sense, more often than not, *why* is the question people embrace, as if it will bring comfort. The problem with this question is that it is not often accompanied by an answer.

Asking a question that may never be answered creates a breeding ground for doubt, bitterness, frustration, and unbelief. Choosing to embrace the question *why* will allow doubt, bitterness, frustration, and unbelief to reign. There is no faith in that question. There is no peace. There is no joy. *Why* is the garden in which failure grows—but failure was not an option in the midst of my tragedy.

Paul affirmed tragedy would be part of life as a believer. Any situation is powerless outside of the love of God. Paul wrote:

> *Who shall separate us from the love of Christ? Shall trouble or hardship or persecution or famine or nakedness or danger or sword? As it is written:*
>
> *"For your sake we face death all day long; we are considered as sheep to be slaughtered."*
>
> *No, in all these things we are more than conquerors through him who loved us.*
>
> *For I am convinced that neither death nor life, neither angels nor demons, neither the present nor the future, nor any powers, neither height nor depth, nor anything else in all*

creation, will be able to separate us from the love of God that is in Christ Jesus our Lord." — **Romans 8:35–39 (NIV)**

Paul declared one of the greatest promises in the Bible: *Nothing can separate you from the love of God.* No attempts to separate you from God's love will be successful—as long you don't get caught up in the *why* of Satan's attempts to divide.

As soon as you begin asking "Why?" your eyes drift from Jesus to the problem, which has the potential of causing doubt. Followers of Jesus have an adversary who would love nothing more than for believers' trials to be what draws them away from faith.

Over the years, I have talked with several people who could never get over the *why*. I remember a man who came into my office and began to rant, "Why does God let children die of cancer? Why does God allow terrorists to kill people? Why do kids get molested? Why do people die young?" I felt so bad for this person because he had been completely overcome by the *why*.

The first thing I reminded him, and something of which everyone needs to be reminded, is that God is not the author of those terrible things. This guy was mad at God and holding Him responsible for all the injustice in the world. But the truth is God is a good and just God who is not the author of injustice and tragedy. As Deuteronomy 32:4 says, "His work is perfect, For all His ways are just; a God of faithfulness and without injustice, righteous and upright is He" (NASB). God is perfectly just, fair, righteous, and perfect.

Those who trust in God trust Him as the One who rights all injustice. God is not the author of your tragedy, but He is the One who will cause good to come from it (see Romans 8:28). God did not make you sick. God did not cause that accident. God did not kill anyone. Those are the kind of thoughts the enemy puts in people's minds when they embrace the question *why.*

On the contrary, God is good. He is for you, and He loves you. One day every believer will stand before Him (2 Corinthians 5:10) and their questions will be answered, but today is not that day. Today is the day to trust in the Lord with all of your heart.

The second thing I told this man, as he sat across from me and demanded to know why terrible things happen, involved a simple answer. It was an answer that pride and flesh hates, and it comes in three little words: "I don't know."

I don't know why that child died. I don't know why that person ran a stop sign. I don't know why your husband left you. I don't know! Sometimes there is an answer, but sometimes there's not. That is why Solomon said it is not wise to ask that question. It will eat a person up because sometimes there is simply no answer.

Stop "*why*-ning." Stop asking the wrong questions and start asking the right ones.

Don't Ask Why—Ask "Who?"

What, then, is the right question? King David, who wrote many of the psalms, had insight into a better query when facing tragedy:

> *Who is this King of glory? The LORD strong and mighty, the LORD mighty in battle. Lift up your heads, you gates; lift them up, you ancient doors, that the King of glory may come in. Who is he, this King of glory? The LORD Almighty—he is the King of glory.* — **Psalm 24:8–10 (NIV)**

David said "Who?" is a much better question than "Why?" It is impossible for people to focus on what they don't know. But believers can focus on the One they *do* know—Jesus. They know the King of glory, who is powerful and able to fight the battle they can't.

I know who my God is. The better I come to know who Jesus is, the more triumphant I will be in the midst of tragedy. Difficult times are not opportunities to blame or become angry at God, but rather to deepen your relationship with Him. These are times to depend on Him more than you ever have before in your life.

Now I don't embrace *why*. Instead, I embrace Jesus.

Throughout the Old Testament, God revealed His character, His divine nature. Focus on God's nature rather than the *why* of your situation. Some examples of God's unfailing character—who He is—that I embrace include:[5]

- "El Elyon," the most High God

- "Jehovah-Nissi," the Lord my Banner
- "Elohim," God
- "Jehovah Shalom," the Lord is Peace
- "El Shaddai," Lord God Almighty
- "Adonai," Lord, Master
- "El Roi," the God who sees me [6]
- "Jehovah Mekoddishkem," the Lord who sanctifies you
- "Jehovah Jireh," the Lord will Provide
- "Jehovah Raah," the Lord my Shepherd
- "Jehovah Rapha," the Lord that Heals
- "Jehovah Shammah," the Lord is There
- "Jehovah Tsidkenu," the Lord Our Righteousness

In this season of uncertainty, you can be confident of who your God is. He is the One who will be enough to carry you through the tragedy—who will provide, heal, and never leave you. As your Shepherd, He will bring you peace and ensure you will be sanctified (made more holy) through your darkest days. His desire is for your life.

Focusing on Jesus is far better than asking "Why?"—and the results are eternal.

But asking "Who?" isn't the only question believers can pose during tragedy—they can also ask "What?" It may feel like a riskier question than "Who?" but asking "What?" is paramount in the midst of a trial. This is the question that will lead to transformation.

Don't Ask Why—Ask "What?"

In trying times, it is vital that believers ask God what He wants to do in them as a result of the tragedy. I will admit that upon learning I had cancer, my first reaction wasn't to say, "Okay, Lord, what do You want to do in me?" No, it was to scream *"Why?"*

But the more I humbled myself and sought God's comfort in Scripture to see what the Word said concerning people facing difficulty, I saw example after example of lives changed amidst trials.

Even Jesus opened Himself up to what God wanted to do during His darkest hour. "Abba, Father," [Jesus] said, "everything is possible for you. Take this cup from me. Yet not what I will, but what you will" (Mark 14:36 NIV, emphasis added).

During the most difficult time in Jesus' life, He welcomed what the Father wanted to do in Him and through Him. The right questions look like this:

"Lord, *what* do You want to do in me during this trial?"

"*What* do You want to change in me?"

"*What* do You want me to learn in this situation?"

These are productive questions. They are questions that make the devil tremble because they don't breed doubt and unbelief, but faith and humility. If you ask the right questions, the greatest opportunity for growth comes during the greatest trials. Thus, as James wrote:

Consider it pure joy, my brothers, whenever you face trials of many kinds, because you know that the testing of your faith produces perseverance. Let perseverance finish its work so that you may be mature and complete, not lacking anything. — **James 1:2–4 (NIV)**

In other words, trials are designed to test one's faith, but that testing produces something. Trials are intended to help God's people grow, learn, and mature in the faith. Nobody likes them, but if you are going to go through them, you might as well embrace the benefits.

A Breakdown and an Unexpected Call

After asking "Why?" for a period of time, I began to see the manifestation of that question's destructive power.

My family and I were attempting to operate as normal for the sake of our kids. So we decided to go to a little carnival on our town square. It was a Thursday evening and we were walking around trying to have fun, but fear had filled my heart.

As I looked around at all of the people, they seemed so happy. I couldn't stop looking at my children and wondering if I would be around the next year to bring them back to the carnival.

Finally, I told my wife that I was starting to freak out and we needed to leave. I didn't know what was happening to me then, but I know now that I was having a panic attack. We no sooner shut the doors to the car than I completely lost it—I freaked out, crying uncontrollably. I wanted to run away. I wanted to hide.

My wife drove us to our church, where the weekly prayer service was about to start, and she helped the kids out of the car. I remember my dad trying to comfort me, but nothing could calm me down.

Finally, I settled down to the point where I could breathe. My family sat with me in the back row of the church.

I knew something had to change. If I kept going like this, I wouldn't have to worry about cancer killing me—fear and depression alone were doing a great job. As I sat in the back row and questioned God, fixating on *why*, the anxiety only grew worse.

Then, completely broken and angry with God, I prayed this prayer: "Lord, *what* do You want to do in me through this trial?"

Immediately I felt a peace come over me that I had never experienced until that point. I knew in that moment there was some kind of purpose for all the pain.

By the time the prayer service ended, I had calmed all the way down, and we headed home. As I walked into the house, my phone rang.

It was my dad. I knew it had been really hard for him to see me have a panic attack, because he had battled anxiety himself for many years. It was just a few years back that he had been completely delivered from anxiety.

He asked me how I was doing, and I could hear the concern in his voice. I knew my dad loved me and would take my place in a moment if he could. He encouraged me, prayed with me, and told me he loved me, and we ended the conversation.

About thirty seconds later, my phone rang. My dad's number flashed on the caller ID again. Assuming he had forgotten to tell me something, I answered. "Hello?" Silence. "Hello?" Still nothing on the other end except a rustling noise. I could tell from the sound my dad had accidentally re-dialed my number without knowing it. I was about to hang the phone up when, all of a sudden, I could hear my dad's voice.

I listened intently to see if I could make out what he was saying. I could tell he was praying. As I continued to listen in, his praying grew louder and I could tell he was praying for *me*.

At first, the prayer was typical. "Lord heal my son. Comfort my son. Give him peace." That kind of stuff. I was very touched to hear my dad praying for me like that. The prayer continued on for about a minute, and then there was silence.

After a few seconds of silence, his calm and typical prayer radically changed. He was screaming!

This prayer wasn't like the one moments earlier. This one was full of passion, anger, and emotion. In all my life I had never heard my dad like this. He was weeping, yelling, laughing, and speaking in tongues all at the same time. It was crazy! He was praying so hard, I almost felt sorry for the devil. To this very day, I have never heard anyone else pray like that.

Just when I thought it couldn't go to another level, he began banging on something! I don't know what it was, but I felt sorry for whatever it was, too.

On the other end of the line, tears began to roll down my cheeks. To know someone loved me so much was profoundly touching.

Then followed another silence-filled pause.

Supposing he was finished, I was about to hang up, but suddenly he began to pray again. This time all the anger was gone, but desperation and brokenness were attached to his words. He began to repeat the same phrase, "God, spare my son!" Over and over he repeated those words. I was weeping and couldn't take anymore. I hung up the phone.

I was utterly stunned by my dad's love for me. An overwhelming feeling of gratefulness overcame me. I couldn't believe my father loved me so much he would pray for me like that! Those words, "God, spare my son," repeated like a broken record in my head.

At that moment, I heard the voice of the Lord whisper to me these words: "Kolbe, I spared not my son." Those words aligned with the truth Paul wrote in Romans 8:32:

He that spared not his own Son, but delivered him up for us all, how shall he not with him also freely give us all things?
(KJV)

That truth hit me like a ton of bricks. As much as my natural father wanted me to be okay, my heavenly Father wanted it so much more. My earthly father was not willing to "spare his son," but for my sake, my heavenly Father had "spared not His own son"! The revelation of

God's intense love for me became more real in that moment than it had ever been before.

I remembered the prayer I had prayed just an hour earlier: "Lord, what do You want to do in me during this trial?" In the first hour of opening myself up to God's purpose, He had already shown me part of the *what*. Already, out of this terrible tragedy had come a revelation of His love like never before.

God showed me that if I would take my eyes off of the *why* and keep them on the *what*, then He could bring purpose to my pain. He could bring a testimony out of the test. Overhearing my father's prayer solidified my understanding of how much God wanted me to be healed—*more than I wanted to be healed*. God had given His best for me, and that meant I was valuable to Him.

When you understand how much God loves you, your confidence begins to grow in *His* ability to take care of you. Asking *what* God wanted to do through me was the beginning—and it was far more critical than asking *why*.

Don't Ask Why—Ask "How?"

God's method of deliverance has not changed. It is just as effective today as it was two thousand years ago. The precious blood of Jesus spilt on Calvary's cross is what delivers God's people. Faith in the power of the blood of Christ is how you are going to make it through this difficulty in your life. Asking how God delivers is more important than asking why something is happening.

Ephesians 1:7 proclaims how God delivers: "In him we have redemption through his blood, the forgiveness of sins, in accordance with the riches of God's grace" (NIV). The riches of God's grace are found in the blood of Jesus.

God's mighty method of deliverance always has been and always will be the answer for every difficult situation. Whether the problem is sin, sickness, doubt, or fear, the blood of Jesus' life-giving sacrifice is the answer.

His blood is how God is going to bring you through this season, but you have to embrace its power, just like when you trusted its power to wash away your every sin when you first came to Christ. Fully trust that it is able to cleanse you from sin, sickness, fear, and doubt. Jesus freely laid down His life so that everyone who was willing could receive the life-changing power of His precious blood.

Only One Treatment

I learned so much about cancer after I was diagnosed that I hadn't known before. I was thrown into a world that I had no clue even existed up until that point.

One of the things I discovered is that for every type of cancer, there was a certain drug to treat it. The drug that works on colon cancer doesn't work on breast cancer, and the one that works on breast cancer doesn't work on lung cancer.

I met a lady who had breast cancer during one of my many trips to the oncologist. She shared her story of being diagnosed and her treatment protocol, which involved a mastectomy followed by a certain type of chemo and radiation. She immediately went into remission and was well for about a year until the cancer returned.

My heart broke for this woman as I asked her what the next step was. She told me her doctors had to try a new type of drug because her cancer was no longer responding to the original one. She was devastated because she thought her remission meant she was going to be okay. But remission doesn't mean the cancer is gone. Rather, it means the cancer is responding to the current treatment given and is not growing or spreading any further.

What does this story have to do with the blood of Christ? *Everything.*

There are more than one hundred types of cancers.[7] Just as there are numerous cancers, people face diverse difficulties. While one person may be facing a divorce, another might have experienced a death in the family. Still another might have a terminal illness. But unlike cancer, God doesn't have a different "drug" for each one. He only has one—the blood of Jesus. Jesus' blood treats broken hearts as well as doubt. His blood treats addiction, but also fear.

Consider what Peter said in Acts 2:38: "Then Peter said unto them, Repent, and be baptized every one of you in the name of Jesus Christ for the *remission* of sins, and ye shall receive the gift of the Holy Ghost" (KJV, emphasis added).

Peter's choice of words is quite interesting—Jesus' name brings "remission" for sin. The word 'remission' in the Greek means "release or freedom from bondage or imprisonment" or "pardon of sins."[8] Thus, Acts 2:38 does not mean sin has been eradicated from the earth, but that a person who receives Jesus as his or her Savior can have freedom from the power of sin.

Recall that in medical terms, remission doesn't mean a disease is gone. Rather, remission means that because of treatment, the disease is not growing or spreading. Peter was not denying the existence of sin in Acts 2:38, but rejoicing in the fact that the power of sin has been broken in people who have been born again by His precious blood.

I love what the writer of Psalm 91 said:

> *A thousand shall fall at thy side, and ten thousand at thy right hand; but it shall not come nigh thee. Only with thine eyes shalt thou behold and see the reward of the wicked. Because thou hast made the LORD, which is my refuge, even the most High, thy habitation; there shall no evil befall thee, neither shall any plague come nigh thy dwelling.*
> *— Psalm 91:7–10 (KJV)*

The chaos of sin and circumstance might surround you, but they cannot come "nigh thy dwelling." The blood is God's chosen method of deliverance, and everything must respond to its presence.

If fear is what you are facing, tell fear it has to face the blood of Jesus. If it's depression, tell it to face the blood. When you do, those issues will begin to respond to God's prescribed treatment.

When I was first diagnosed, the cancer wasn't my biggest problem. My biggest problems were the fear, doubt, and unbelief that came with it. The more revelation I received about how God was going to carry me through my illness, the more the spiritual tumors of doubt, fear and unbelief began to shrink. And as I continued to walk out my faith, they ultimately were eradicated in my life.

As you trust the power of the blood, every circumstance in your life—both spiritual and natural—must respond because it is God's mighty chosen method of deliverance. Declare today that sin, sickness, disease, depression, addiction, fear, and doubt are in remission because of the blood.

Stand Firm, Full of Faith

The apostle Paul faced trial after trial as he obeyed God and carried the gospel to the world. He was beaten, imprisoned, shipwrecked, and persecuted—certainly, he understood tragedy.

However, Paul placed his hope in Jesus so that he might be able to continue to do what God had called him to do. Perhaps this was why he passionately exhorted the Corinthian church to "stand firm in the faith; be courageous; be strong" (1 Corinthians 16:13 NIV).

As you walk through this difficulty in your life, make sure you are asking the right questions. *Why* will only leave you empty and frustrated. But *who, what,* and *how* will leave you full of faith so that you can stand firm and move forward to greater days ahead.

WORKBOOK

Chapter 6 Questions

Question: What questions have you asked during your times of great difficulty and trial?

_____

_____

_____

_____

_____

_____

_____

_____

_____

_____

_____

Question: What questions should you be asking in your situation? What are the answers?

_____

_____

_____

_____

_____

_____

_____

_____

_____

_____

_____

_____

Action: Don't cry out "Why?" in despair at your current difficulties. Instead, focus on *who* you need (Jesus), *what* He is accomplishing through you and for you, and *how* He will carry you to victory (by His blood). As you stand firm, full of faith, declare that sin, sickness and disease, depression, addiction, and fear are in remission in your life!

Chapter 6 Notes

_____

_____

_____

_____

_____

_____

_____

_____

_____

_____

_____

_____

_____

_____

_____

_____

_____

_____

_____

_____

_____

_____

_____

_____

_____

CHAPTER SEVEN

Confronting the Bullies

Confrontation is messy.

It's unpleasant and uncomfortable. It requires you to say things other people don't want to hear. It's not especially nice.

It involves sticking your neck out—and possibly making a scene.

Yet it's also absolutely essential to human growth.

If you are like me, you want to avoid confrontation at all costs. You want to keep the peace and not ruffle any feathers.

But being a pastor, I don't always have that luxury. In fact, if you are in any kind of position of leadership, confrontation is a part of your everyday life. Without confrontation, people don't change—they don't grow, and they can't move forward.

Spiritual Bullies

When I was in the seventh grade, there was a class bully. I realize that that word 'bully' carries particular moral and psychological connotations in this day and age, but back then nobody seemed to care. There were no seminars preaching the anti-bullying gospel—we just had to deal with it.

Nonetheless, this young man was a jerk in every sense of the word. He had gone through puberty at an earlier age than everyone else, so he was twice the size of all the other guys in my class. He terrorized everyone. We kept our lunch money in our underwear, because that was the only place it was safe. (The money got a little gross when he gave us wedgies, though.)

My friends and I would get together and have secret meetings about confronting him, but no one ultimately had the courage to do anything except complain and whine, which is all people can do if they choose not to be confrontational.

This bully and I had opposite lunch times, so when I was going to lunch, he was returning. He would always push me off the sidewalk. It infuriated me! I would lie in bed at night and think of what I could do.

One day I worked up the courage to push him back. I had it all planned out: he would push me as usual, but this time I would respond with a powerful shove of my own. I knew it would probably cost me my life, but I didn't care. I was fed up.

The bully walked toward me, and our eyes fixed on each other. Usually I would not make eye contact with him, but this time I stood my ground and didn't even blink. I was playing out the next few seconds in my mind and bracing for the impact of his shove. "This is my moment," I thought. Then everything went black.

I awoke on the ground with a bunch of kids standing over me and laughing. The bully was leading the pack, of course.

While focusing on my eye contact with the guy, I forgot to pay attention to where I was walking. I had walked directly into one of the poles on the covered walkway and knocked myself out. Needless to say, it was a confrontation fail.

After that, I decided that I was not the hero of seventh grade who was going to put the guy in his place. However, someone still needed to confront this bully and put an end to his terrorism.

At last the day came. It was a Friday and school had just let out. My friends and I were talking in front of the school, waiting for our parents to pick us up. The bully walked up and we all knew he was going to mess with us.

He set his crosshairs on one of my friends, pulling his backpack off his shoulders and causing it to fall to the ground. Nobody said a word, and I was expecting my buddy to take it as usual. Much to our surprise, my friend asked the bully to stop.

Now, you need to understand something about my friend. He was one hundred pounds soaking wet, and was the least likely of all of us to be able to stand up to this maniac. That's why we were so shocked when he said something.

The bully was just as shocked as we were, so he pushed my friend again and challenged him to do something about it. That is when it happened. My friend reached back as far as he could and with an open hand slapped the bully as hard as he could right in the face. I will never forget the sound of my friend's open palm smacking against that guy's face. It was beautiful.

We all stood completely silent, paralyzed by awe and fear. We were terrified of what was about to happen to our friend.

But to our amazement, the guy didn't tear our friend's head off. No, he stood just as paralyzed as the rest of us. Tears began to fill the bully's eyes and roll down his cheeks. His bottom lip slowly began to poke out and quiver. In a whimpering voice, he brokenly asked my friend, "Why did you do that?"

Goliath had fallen! My buddy had confronted the bully. He had called the bully's bluff and won. The bully apologized to my friend, they shook hands, and seventh grade was forever changed. Why? Because my friend finally confronted our oppressor.

I tell this story because when going through a tragedy, there are several big and scary things that will try to push you around. These are things that you, like my friend, will have to confront. They will try to control you, and they will seem too big to handle. Yet just as my friend did with the bully in the seventh grade, you can call their bluff.

I like to call these things the "Deadly D's." These Deadly D's rear their ugly heads in the midst of a tragedy, and it is crucial to confront these spiritual bullies to experience victory.

Deadly D #1: Denial

In the early days of my diagnosis, people would always ask me how I was doing and my response was always the same: "I'm fine." That obviously couldn't have been further from the truth. I wasn't fine. The shock had worn off and I was afraid, angry, and uncertain, but the bully of denial was pushing me around.

I have talked to so many people going through a difficult time, and their response is the same as mine: "I'm fine."

How can you find out your spouse has been cheating, a child is sick, a loved one has died, or you were diagnosed with cancer, and still be fine? You can't! You are in denial, and as long as you are there, you can't face the difficulty and move forward. Denial can be dangerous because the longer you refuse to look at the reality of your situation, the harder it will be when you finally do.

Many Christians mistake denial for faith and strength. I have heard so many people pray about a tragic situation, whether it be theirs or someone else's, and say: "I refuse to believe it."

Picture someone who has broken their arm. Despite the fact that the bone is sticking out, what if they said, "I refuse to believe it"? That is not faith. That is not strong. That is stupid. Healing in that arm can't begin until the person comes to grip with the fact that it's broken. The truth is, if they wait a couple of days before they deal with the break, it is going to be a lot more difficult to fix than if they went to doctor as soon as they broke it.

I know this because when I was fifteen it happened to me. I was riding on the back of my buddy's four-wheeler one night and wound up breaking both bones in my left arm. I knew that I had broken it because of the pain and swelling, but I didn't want to believe it.

You see, it happened during my baseball all-star season. I knew that if my arm was broken, my baseball season was over. So instead of getting my arm fixed, I lied and told my parents, "I'm fine."

Finally, a few days later, I was in so much pain that I told my parents the truth. They immediately took me to the doctor, who confirmed the break. The only problem was, the bones had already begun to heal.

I will never forget when the doctor called in several other large male doctors and nurses. He asked my mom to leave the room and informed my dad and me that he was going to have to re-break the arm so he could set it and the arm could heal properly.

I wasn't very excited about the idea, so I bolted for the nearest exit, but I was no match for the five large men. I looked to my dad for rescue, but he had a strange look of satisfaction on his face. Then I realized, he had probably wanted to break my arm for a long time.

As the men held me down, the doctor put my arm over his knee and literally re-broke it. It was one of the worst experiences of my life. At that point all I could think about was how I wished I had gone to the doctor right away. Denial had bullied me into thinking I was fine, but I wasn't.

I can't count the number of people I have met who choose to ignore their pain for years. And when they finally chose to deal with it, they had to re-break that area in their lives.

Why live with that kind of unnecessary pain? Why waste all that time being pushed around by denial? Real faith doesn't say, "I am fine," but rather, "I'm fighting."

Real strength isn't found in being strong, but in weakness and complete dependence on Jesus. Paul taught this in 2 Corinthians 12:9 when he affirmed Jesus' grace was "sufficient for thee: for my strength is made perfect in weakness" (KJV).

Paul knew when he was weak and wholly depending on Christ, he was strong. The day you quit refusing to believe you are in the situation you are in, and instead you begin to fight, is the day your healing will begin. That is the day you will be strong.

Deadly D #2: Depression

Probably the meanest of all of the bullies that show up in the midst of tragedy is depression. Up until my diagnosis, I didn't really understand much about depression. I had always been a pretty happy and carefree kind of person. When I gave my life to Jesus, I somehow knew and believed God had my life under His control.

That's why the numbness of depression was a new experience for me. The sense of not being able to see or feel anything outside of my own circumstance was something I had never undergone, and it was scary.

My pastor once described depression as being in a large well-lit room with many people and much activity going on. When depression sets in, the lights begin to dim until the only light in the room is a tight beam focused on the person suffering from depression. Despite the fact there are many other people present and bustling activity, the depressed person only sees themselves. The spotlight of focus rests only on them.

This was where I was in the early weeks after my tragedy. I was in a world of other people and circumstances, but I couldn't see them. Depression centered my focus on my own problems. All I could think about was *my* sickness, *my* family, and *my* fate.

It is never healthy to focus only on yourself, even when there is no tragedy. To be honest, the sickness of depression was worse than the actual disease I was fighting. It was like drowning in a dark ocean and being able to see a flickering light just above the water's surface. No matter how hard I tried to swim up to reach the light, I only sank further down.

Let's revisit the story of Elijah. In 1 Kings 18, Elijah proved his God was the one true God, and then he killed 450 prophets of Baal. It was a great victory for the Lord!

That was, until Queen Jezebel sent Elijah a message in 1 Kings 19:2 saying she was going to kill him for what he had done. This same man who had fearlessly stood in the face of 450 men decided to run for his life from one woman, Jezebel.

I can sympathize with Elijah, because I know what it feels like for something evil to threaten my life. The sad part of the story was how Elijah responded to the bully—

not to Jezebel, but to depression, which is equally a bully. Elijah wound up in a cave all alone with the spotlight of depression shining bright on him. Read what he said when the Lord spoke to him:

There he went into a cave and spent the night.

And the word of the LORD came to him: "What are you doing here, Elijah?"

He replied, "I have been very zealous for the LORD God Almighty. The Israelites have rejected your covenant, torn down your altars, and put your prophets to death with the sword. I am the only one left, and now they are trying to kill me too." — 1 Kings 19:9–10 (NIV)

Elijah was in a cave alone, singing the song of the depressed. "I am the only one who is going through this," he lamented, "I am the only one who feels this way." If you are voicing any of those phrases, I can assure you the bully of depression is messing with you.

God continued, telling Elijah he *wasn't* the only one standing for Him, but that there were seven thousand others (1 Kings 19:18). God turned the light on in the rest of the room. Some people need God to turn the light on for them before they realize they are not the only ones going through difficulty.

I remember the night God illuminated the dark room I camped in. I was depressed. My thoughts were self-focused. My words were about myself and my problems. When I prayed, it was all about me. It was as if everyone and everything else ceased to exist. I was in depression's spotlight. I was in Elijah's cave.

My church hosts a weekly prayer meeting on Monday nights. It is customary to go to the front and pray, and many times people will gather around in support and lay hands on the person for whom they're praying.

This particular night, I went up for prayer. The prayer I prayed was for myself, of course. It must have been a pretty sad and depressing prayer, because the whole congregation came up to surround and pray for me. They sat me down in a chair and began to intercede. I wasn't listening to their prayers at all, but simply feeling sorry for myself.

My church also regularly anoints the sick with oil. My pastor loves Israel and has been there several times. Each time he goes, he brings back anointing oil. This isn't the average olive oil in a pretty glass container found at most churches. No, this stuff is stout. It's like the Ever Clear of anointing oil. Just a small drop can fill the whole church with its fragrance.

As the people were praying for me, I smelled that all-too-familiar smell of imported oil. I had already been anointed with oil several times, so I didn't quite understand why they were doing it again, but I really didn't care as long as it was all about me.

It was in that moment I felt something warm on top of my head. I wasn't sure what it was, but I heard one of the ladies say, "Oh my, that is too much." Then I heard others laugh quietly. By this time the warm feeling had begun to run down my entire head and the smell of anointing oil filled the room. It was then I realized what had happened. The entire bottle of oil had been poured on top of my head. The oil filled both of my ears and ran down my back.

At this point, all I wanted to do was find out who was at fault so I could punch them in the face. As soon as I opened my eyes, however, oil oozed into my eyes.

The only pain I can relate to this was the time my dad accidently squirted gasoline in my eyes at a gas station when I was a kid. I couldn't hear, I couldn't see, and my entire body was greasy. I was so embarrassed, and I grew angry. I went to the bathroom to clean up the best I could before coming back to join the prayer service. The whole experience took about half an hour.

As I sat back down, I heard someone praying. I realized that was the longest I had gone since my diagnosis without thinking about it. For weeks I had only thought of myself. The bully of depression had been pushing me around without me even realizing it.

I listened to the woman's prayers: she prayed for her prodigal son who was experiencing terrible times. My heart broke for her and her situation. It felt so good to feel something for someone besides myself. God had turned on the light. I wasn't the only one going through something.

I went from wanting to kill the guy who poured oil in my eyes to wanting to hug him. It took God pouring oil in my eyes to pull me out of my funk. I had finally embraced Paul's words: while "for those who are self-seeking and who reject the truth and follow evil, there will be wrath and anger" (Romans 2:8 NIV), I was now choosing to be selfless and think of others as better than myself (Philippians 2:3 NLT).

The greatest way to fight depression is to do something for someone beside yourself. Pray for someone beside yourself. Think of someone beside yourself. Find someone who is going through a similar situation and reach out to them with the love of God.

Depression wants to keep you from fulfilling your purpose in this season, but you don't have to let it. Confront the bully of depression.

Deadly D #3: Discontentment

Last but not least is discontentment. This bully always shows up in the midst of difficult times. Simply put, discontentment is the longing for circumstances other than one's own. It seems natural in the midst of trying times to want different circumstances, but if you're not careful, this can prove to be very dangerous.

I remember how this bully pushed me around in the early days of my tragedy. Up until this point in my life, I had been very content. I had a beautiful wife, great kids, and a nice house, and I loved my job. Never had I looked around wanting something other than what God had given me. This all changed when the reality of losing all those things set in.

Rachel sent me to the grocery store one afternoon after we returned from a doctor's appointment. I will never forget the feeling of desperately wanting to be one of the many strangers I saw in the store. It was terrible. My heart filled with envy and jealousy with each person I looked at. In that moment, I was sure that every one of those strangers had circumstances better than mine, and I couldn't help the overwhelming feeling that I would trade places with them if I could.

Looking back on it, it seems silly. If I had the ability to step into each one of their circumstances, I would have experienced a rude awakening, because everyone is dealing with their own set of difficulties. But discontentment had overtaken me.

The Bible has much to say about discontentment, otherwise known as coveting. The meaning of the word 'covet' is to crave for something other than what one has.[9]

Americans are great at doing this. And they don't need to have a tragedy to long for something they don't have. They are good at coveting when things are going great, too! When someone gets a raise at a job, they long more for the car their neighbor just bought. When they get the car, they want the boat. And it goes on and on.

The Word of God speaks sharply against this: "You shall not covet your neighbor's house. You shall not covet your neighbor's wife, or his male or female servant, his ox or donkey, or anything that belongs to your neighbor" (Exodus 20:17 NIV).

But coveting occurs just as much during difficult times—and it's important to be guarded against desiring what others have that you might not. Longing for health because your neighbor doesn't have an illness, and wanting his life rather than your own, is coveting what you don't have.

The New Testament warns against coveting, too. Romans 13:9 says, "The commandments, 'You shall not commit adultery,' 'You shall not murder,' 'You shall not steal,' 'You shall not covet,' and whatever other command there may be, are summed up in this one command: 'Love your neighbor as yourself'" (NIV). Coveting what others have, even health, negates God's command to love others.

The answer in the midst of a trial isn't to crave someone else's circumstances, but to reach down deep and depend on what God has placed in you: His love. Then, instead of coveting what your neighbor has, you will love them for who they are.

God has given you everything you need to make it through this trial. You don't need to crave what someone else has! Instead, long for the great things God has in store for you—His peace, His joy, His healing, His comfort, and His transformative love. As Second Peter 1:3 says, "According as his divine power hath given unto us all things that *pertain* unto life and godliness, through the knowledge of him that hath called us to glory and virtue" (KJV).

When you are tempted to look at others who are not experiencing tragedy and long for their situation instead of your own, remember Paul's words to the Philippian church:

*Finally, brethren, whatsoever things are true, whatsoever things **are** honest, whatsoever things **are** just, whatsoever things **are** pure, whatsoever things **are** lovely, whatsoever things **are** of good report; if **there be** any virtue, and if **there be** any praise, think on these things. — **Philippians 4:8 (KJV, emphasis added)***

Think on the things of God—things that are pure and lovely—and He will be faithful to remove your longing for other things. This is how to destroy the bully of discontentment.

No matter what difficulty you are facing, be confident that these bullies—denial, depression, and discontentment—will show up and try to push you around. But just as my friend in the seventh grade stood up to the class bully, you too must stand up to the Deadly D's and fight for the victory available to you through the blood of Christ.

Those bullies can't control you, because the Word of God is stronger and dwells within you (1 Corinthians 3:16). Don't take the abuse lying down! Instead, as we read in God's Word: "Stand firm and you will see the deliverance the LORD will bring" (Exodus 14:13 NIV).

WORKBOOK

Chapter 7 Questions

Question: How, specifically, are the three Deadly D's manifesting in your trial and trying to suppress your hope and faith?

_____

_____

_____

_____

_____

_____

_____

_____

_____

_____

_____

Question: How exactly will you confront, overcome, and banish each of the Deadly D's in your situation?

_____

_____

_____

_____

_____

_____

_____

_____

_____

_____

_____

_____

_____

Action: Deny any place to the Deadly D's of denial, depression, and discontentment! Instead of dwelling on these three spiritual bullies, think on pure, lovely, and godly things that bolster your hope and faith.

Chapter 7 Notes

CHAPTER EIGHT

The Highway of "Missing It"

Along my driveway, leading up to the front door of my house, there is a flowerbed on the left side of the sidewalk. I use the term 'flowerbed' loosely here, because my wife and I are not known for our landscaping skills. To be honest, it's more like a dirt bed dotted with old rotting leaves.

But in the midst of the dirt and decaying leaves is a cute little stone etched with the phrase, "Stop and smell the flowers." I love that stone because without fail, every time we pass by it, my kids stop and start sniffing. It doesn't matter how big of a hurry we are in, how many bags of groceries I am carrying, or how mad I get, they always stop and smell the flowers. This is how the conversation usually unfolds when they stop and smell these non-existing flowers:

Me: Girls! Go! We are in a hurry!

Girls: …

The girls keep sniffing as if I had never spoken.

Me: Move!

Girls: What dad? The rock says to stop and smell the flowers. That is what we are doing.

Me: There aren't any flowers.

Girls: Dad, it doesn't matter. We are just doing what the rock says.

Me: I wish what I said was as important as what the rock says.

The drama at this point can't possibly be documented accurately on paper.

Girls: Wow, Dad. You ruin everything. Why are you always in such a hurry?

At this point in the ritual, I feel like the worst dad in the world, so the three of us spend the next five minutes sniffing dirt and rotten leaves.

If you are a parent—especially of girls—I know you can identify with me. But seriously, there is much value in this story. So often in the midst of trying times it is easy to avoid smelling the flowers.

I am not suggesting everything you are going through is all rosy, but I am suggesting there is value in taking time to enjoy what is still beautiful while in this dark season. The tendency to want to fast forward through all the pain and heartache to a place of normalcy can overshadow some of the lovely things God has for you now.

Embrace and Enjoy the Journey

I can remember going through this exact thing—I wanted to wake up five years down the road, cancer free with my life back. I don't want to contradict what I have written in previous chapters about having vision, because yes, it is important to see yourself victorious and on the other side of this struggle. However, that doesn't mean there won't be value in every day of the journey to get there.

King David wrote, "This is the day the Lord has made; let us rejoice and be glad in it" (Psalm 118:24 NKJV). God created every day, and regardless of your circumstances, His Word says to rejoice and be glad in it. This doesn't apply only to the good times, but *all* times.

My daughters did not stop and smell the flowers because there were flowers, but because the rock said to do it. You may feel like all the flowers in life's garden have been pulled up and all that's left is dirt and rotting leaves. You may not feel as if there is anything to rejoice and be glad about today—but do it anyway, because the Word instructs you to do so. During this rough season, God has a treasure for you every step of the way. Don't miss it!

An Angry Monster and Some Sand

A few years ago, I was with my parents in San Diego on business. When we finished, we decided to head up to Los Angeles for a couple of days. As we began our journey in our rented Nissan Versa (the smallest car known to mankind), we pulled onto Interstate 5 for the two-hour drive. If you know anything about the West Coast, you know about I-5. It runs from the border of Tijuana all the way to Canada.

A necessary and important detail about this trip was why I was desperate to arrive in Los Angeles as soon as possible: my mother had decided that day she was going to quit drinking Diet Dr. Pepper.

That may not seem like a big deal, but it is the equivalent of enraging Bruce Banner. Without Diet Dr. Pepper, my mother—like Banner (aka, "The Hulk")—my mother turns into an angry monster that destroys everything in her path.

What made my mother want to quit on this particular day, I don't know, but I do know it was a disaster. All I wanted to do was get to Los Angeles as quickly as possible to find refuge from the monster. After about thirty minutes, she had grown so hateful that I had my dad pull off of I-5 into a store. While I supported my mother's decision to better her health, the more immediate threat to her health was the possibility of me throwing her out of the Nissan Versa.

So I did what any good son would do. I went into the store and returned with a Diet Dr. Pepper. Of course, I did not have to twist the addict's arm. She downed the soda and like magic, the monster was gone and my sweet mother returned.

I was ready to get back on the road and continue to our destination when my dad suggested a shortcut. My dad has a long history of shortcuts, and without fail they are never shorter. He was staring at his phone and pointed out on his GPS that Highway 101 ran parallel with I-5, but right next to the ocean. Interstate 5 is close to the ocean, but just far enough that you can't quite see the water.

I was irritated at his suggestion because I knew exactly what it meant: our two-hour drive was about to turn into five. All I wanted was to get to Los Angeles, but I was stuck in a tiny car with two crazy old people! My mom agreed with my dad, so I was outvoted, and on to Highway 101 we went.

I still remember driving over that hill and seeing the Pacific Ocean in front of me. It was so beautiful. The waves were huge and people were surfing. The road was so close to the water that some of the waves actually ran onto the asphalt a bit.

I don't know how many towns we went through, but each one was like a scene out of the movies. It was by far the most beautiful drive I had ever been on.

We stopped in the town of Oceanside, where my grandfather had been stationed in the military as a young man. We went out onto the beach and dipped our feet in the cool water. It was the perfect day.

While standing on the beach, I turned around and could see the tops of eighteen-wheelers traveling on I-5 about a quarter mile in the distance. I could not believe I-5 was that close, but prevented drivers from experiencing all of the beauty I was enjoying. As I squished the warm sand beneath my toes, I thought, "I can't believe I almost missed this."

The Highway of Missing It

That day was just a few months after I had been diagnosed, and my business in California was cancer treatment. It was on that beach that God revealed to me I was traveling the Highway of Missing It.

I was so desperate to try to outrun the reality of my situation, desperate to hurry past the pain and difficulty. With my feet in the Pacific Ocean, however, I felt God's peace and love as I hadn't in a long time, and the same thought echoed in my brain: "I can't believe I almost missed this."

Peace, love, assurance, healing, and satisfaction weren't five years down the road—they were in that very moment.

God had amazing things for me in every step of my journey with cancer, things He wanted to do *for* me and things He wanted to do *in* me. He had truths He wanted to show me that I could only see in that difficult season. I needed to be broken and vulnerable for them to come into focus.

Tragedy is a place no one wants to be, but no one can avoid. If you are there, don't make the same mistake I did and miss what God has for you—and not just what He has for you, but *don't miss Him!* He is there, and He desperately wants you to know Him in this season of your life.

I have learned through my tragedy, as well as walking with others through theirs, that it is in people's darkest hours when God's light shines the brightest. It is in a person's time of greatest need that they can most clearly see the One who holds the supply for that need. Although I do not enjoy experiencing life's difficulties, I can now testify that tragedy afforded me the opportunity to see God more clearly than ever before.

I know that is a hard thing to read—I know this because it is a hard thing to write. I don't say it so you will live in fear as to what difficulty might lie around the corner, but so you can live in faith and expectation. Rest assured that when the unexpected happens in life, God will be right there and ready to reveal Himself to you as never before.

Would you dare peer through that precious lens your desperate time of need has created and see—really see— your Mighty Deliverer?

Embrace David's declaration:

> *You're blessed when you stay on course, walking steadily on the road revealed by GOD. You're blessed when you follow his directions, doing your best to find them. That's right—you don't go off on your own; you walk straight along the road he set. — Psalm 119:1–2 (MSG)*

Would you dare to believe God has a plan for your desperate situation?

There is an incredible story in 2 Kings 6 that illustrates well what I'm talking about. In 2 Kings 6:8, the King of Aram attempted to ambush the king of Israel, but Elisha—Israel's prophet—revealed the king of Aram's plan to the king of Israel. This happened several times, resulting in a very frustrated king of Aram.

Now the king of Aram was at war with Israel. After confer-
ring with his officers, he said, "I will set up my camp in
such and such a place."

The man of God sent word to the king of Israel: "Beware of
passing that place, because the Arameans are going down
there." So the king of Israel checked on the place indicated
by the man of God. Time and again Elisha warned the king,
so that he was on his guard in such places.

This enraged the king of Aram. He summoned his officers
and demanded of them, "Tell me! Which of us is on the side
of the king of Israel?"

"None of us, my lord the king," said one of his officers,
"but Elisha, the prophet who is in Israel, tells the king of
Israel the very words you speak in your bedroom."

"Go, find out where he is," the king ordered, "so I can
send men and capture him." The report came back: "He is
in Dothan." Then he sent horses and chariots and a strong
force there. They went by night and surrounded the city.

When the servant of the man of God got up and went out
early the next morning, an army with horses and chariots
had surrounded the city. "Oh no, my lord! What shall we
do?" the servant asked. **— 2 Kings 6:8–15 (NIV)**

Have you ever felt like Elisha and his servant? One
day you wake up and everything is fine, but the next day
you are completely surrounded by the enemy. The Bible
says the King of Aram sent a "strong force" to capture
Elisha and his servant. That is exactly what tragedy is—
an unexpected "strong force" that seems to overtake a
person's entire life.

No matter what direction the Israelites looked, they
saw defeat. There was no way of escape. In the natural, it
appeared as if the end was near. I know exactly how the

servant felt, because I have cried that same cry before: "Oh no, Lord! What should we do?"

Facing the dire situation, Elisha didn't panic. He didn't scream and yell "Why?" or sink into a depression. Consider Elisha's response:

> *"Don't be afraid," the prophet answered. "Those who are with us are more than those who are with them."*
>
> *And Elisha prayed, "Open his eyes, LORD, so that he may see." Then the LORD opened the servant's eyes, and he looked and saw the hills full of horses and chariots of fire all around Elisha.* — **2 Kings 6:16–17 (NIV)**

Right in the middle of a terrifying circumstance, Elisha did something that many believers are afraid to do. He didn't get angry with God for allowing the army to find him. He didn't ask God to rescue him. He did not try to negotiate with the army. Rather, he prayed a simple prayer: "LORD, open his eyes that he may see."

Elisha knew his servant was missing something, and he knew that this desperate situation was the perfect opportunity for the servant to see it. It took being completely surrounded with no way of escape, certain defeat, and impending death for the servant to see God in a way he never had before.

It doesn't say this in the Bible, but I would be willing to bet, as the servant's focus changed from Aram's army to the brilliant army of God—as he gazed in awe of the radiant angels and their flaming chariots—he said, "I can't believe I almost missed this."

As soon as the servant's eyes were opened, he could see what he had been missing. In that instant, everything changed. Fear, doubt, and unbelief dissipated and were replaced by faith in his Mighty God.

Would you be so bold to pray that prayer in the midst of *your* situation? "Lord, open my eyes and show me what I have been missing. Let me see You in a way I never have before." Faith will begin to rise in such a way that the strong force working against you will pale in comparison to the mighty force of heaven that is fighting for you.

I bet before Elisha's servant went through this, he believed God could deliver. He had probably heard the story of the children of Israel being delivered from Pharaoh's grip and how they boldly proclaimed, "God can deliver!" His fingers likely moved over the words on the scrolls that retold that story—perhaps he even preached a sermon on it. But that day in Dothan, the servant experienced it. He came to know God as his personal Deliverer.

The God Who Heals...Me

Standing on that beach in Southern California, I resolved not to waste one more day traveling on the Highway of Missing It. At that point in my life, it was still very uncertain how long I had to live. According to the doctors, it was only a few months. I made a decision right then and there that whether I lived a few months or seventy years, I was not going to miss what God had for me, what He wanted to do in me, or what He wanted to accomplish through me.

The reality is that no one is guaranteed another breath, and sometimes it takes a tragedy to realize this. It took the reality of dying to move me off that sorry highway that so many choose to travel in the rat race of life. I am so glad that I did, because I do not miss it any longer. My prayer for you is that you won't, either.

Up until I became sick, I believed God could heal. I had heard of other people being healed. I knew Scriptures about healing. I sang songs about healing. I preached sermons on healing. But it wasn't until I was in a position of needing to be healed that I really came to know Jesus as *my* Healer.

No matter what situation you may be facing, there is a part of God's character that He wants you to know—not because you have heard it or read it, but because you have experienced it. There is beauty where you are now if you are willing to see it. Don't miss it.

Chapter 8 Questions

Question: Where in your life have you found beauty, or where might you find it, amidst your current trial or difficulties?

_____

_____

_____

_____

_____

_____

_____

_____

_____

_____

_____

Question: Beyond believing that God heals, do you know Jesus as your healer? Where does the distinction lie?

_____

_____

_____

_____

_____

_____

_____

_____

_____

_____

_____

_____

Action: Even in unlikely and unenjoyable circumstances, don't miss the beauty of God's handiwork as you come to know Jesus as your personal healer. Instead of resenting your situation, embrace and enjoy the journey God has laid out for you.

Chapter 8 Notes

CHAPTER NINE

Tijuana

Of all the ways and places in the world from which I thought an answer might come, it certainly wasn't a clinic in Tijuana!

Until this point I have shared with you mostly spiritual principles that I learned as I walked through tragedy. However, this chapter will focus on the most practical step I took as I walked toward my miracle.

As I mentioned at the beginning of the book, the doctors had given me only six months to live. There was no hope; there were no viable options. The doctors strongly urged me to begin chemotherapy as soon as possible, but Rachel and I knew we weren't going to do it—we just couldn't. If I only had six months to live, why spend it weak and sick from the treatment?

It had been made very clear to me that even with treatment, I was doomed. My body was riddled with cancer, and there was no cure. The doctors sent us home to think about what we wanted to do and asked us to return in two weeks with a decision.

In those two weeks, Rachel and I prayed and made a decision that would alter not only the outcome of my circumstance, but also the way I understood God.

Divine Connections

Initially, I didn't intend to include this part of my story, but the more I thought about it, the more I realized my story just isn't my story without this chapter.

The reality is that every person's circumstances are ultimately unique. You might be battling with sickness, or maybe you just found out your spouse has been cheating, and your entire world is crashing down around you. Whatever your situation, you must decide how to walk it out both spiritually and in specific, practical terms.

When I was diagnosed, I had to make a thousand practical decisions. What treatment should I choose? What hospital do I go to? How do I deal with missing work? What should I tell my kids? Who watches the kids while Rachel and I are at appointments? How was I going to get the money to pay for it all? The decisions that needed to be made seemed endless!

Of all the practical decisions I made, however, the most difficult came when I received a phone call one evening from a ministry friend. The last time we had spoken was about a year earlier, when she was fighting a cancer battle of her own. She filled me in on how she was doing and some of the steps she had taken since we last talked.

You never know when you will experience one of those divine connections that will alter the course of your life. I definitely wasn't expecting to encounter such a connection as I sat on the phone in my living room, eating a bowl of mac 'n' cheese! But that is exactly how it happened.

As in my case, her doctors had given her very little hope. But she explained to me that after a lot of research, she had chosen to go to a cancer clinic in Tijuana, Mexico.

What?

"Isn't it dangerous? Doesn't El Chapo live there? Did they ask you to smuggle drugs back across the border?" These were just a few of the ridiculous questions I asked her almost mockingly. She just laughed, much as I do now when people ask me the same questions.

However, as I listened to her story of a tumor the size of an orange completely disappearing over the course of a year and her stage four cancer seemingly gone, I was intrigued. In fact, the conversation became so serious that I let my macaroni grow cold, which if you know me is nothing to be taken lightly.

I listened to her talk about her adventure in Mexico for about an hour, until I had asked all the questions I could think of. Then I hung up the phone, not quite sure how I felt. I was confused, overwhelmed, and a little hopeful all at the same time.

Yet as I sat there staring at my cold, half-eaten bowl of macaroni, I felt a peace deep down inside and knew that this was God leading me.

Plan B

I shared everything with Rachel, and after talking to our parents and the clinic in Mexico, we made the decision for me to go.

And that is when it happened—two different people on two separate occasions asked me the same question: "Kolbe, why do you have to go to Mexico for healing? Don't you believe God can heal you here?"

I couldn't be too mad at them, because I had been asking myself the same question. That question said a lot more than the nineteen words that made it up. Here is what it really was suggesting:

"If you really had faith, you would already be healed."

"God doesn't need Mexico to heal you."

"You don't really trust God."

I didn't realize it then, but the box I had created for God was being challenged on every side. Not only was my box was being challenged, but also the box of some of the people around me. Having been raised up in a faith-filled church that believes God still heals just as He did when Jesus walked the earth, there was a certain unspoken expectation when people were sick: if you had the right amount of faith and had rid yourself of all known sin, then God would supernaturally heal you.

So you can imagine how I felt when that didn't happen for me. Many faith-filled people had laid hands on me, just the way the Bible describes. They had prayed all the right prayers, but I was still sick—and filled with shame. I didn't see going to Mexico as God's best answer for my life, but as a sort of Plan B.

In Plan A, which fit inside of my box, I would have received the terrible report, but would then have been miraculously healed. When I returned to the doctor, the scans would have been clear! I never would have had to consider going to Mexico or anywhere else, because God would have already accomplished the miracle.

But Plan A didn't happen. The scans weren't clear, and I did have to go to Mexico.

The unspoken grading system in my world at that time looked something like this:

A = After laying of hands on you, you recover. Period.

B = After you pray and repent of your sin, God heals you.

C = You go to the doctor and get medicine.

F = You go to the doctor in Mexico.

So according to the box in which I'd placed God, and its grading system, I had failed with a big fat F! It hurts me deeply now to think that I viewed God as only being limited to one way of healing me. I don't want you to get me wrong—I do believe we can lay hands on the sick and see them recover instantaneously. I do believe in, and have seen God do, creative miracles that would have fit in my box. I simply no longer believe He is limited only to that method.

Dunked in the River

According to the Bible, there once was a Syrian general named Naaman who suffered from leprosy. And like me, he tried to put God in a box.

Naaman heard that Elisha, Israel's prophet, could heal him:

> *So Naaman with his horses and chariots arrived in style and stopped at Elisha's door.*
>
> *Elisha sent out a servant to meet him with this message: "Go to the River Jordan and immerse yourself seven times. Your skin will be healed and you'll be as good as new."*
>
> *Naaman lost his temper. He turned on his heel saying, "I thought he'd personally come out and meet me, call on the name of GOD, wave his hand over the diseased spot, and get rid of the disease. The Damascus rivers, Abana and Pharpar, are cleaner by far than any of the rivers in Israel. Why not bathe in them? I'd at least get clean." He stomped off, mad as a hornet.*
>
> *But his servants caught up with him and said, "Father, if the prophet had asked you to do something hard and heroic, wouldn't you have done it? So why not this simple 'wash and be clean'?"*
>
> *So he did it. He went down and immersed himself in the Jordan seven times, following the orders of the Holy Man. His skin was healed; it was like the skin of a little baby. He was as good as new.* — *2 Kings 5:9–14(MSG)*

Naaman *thought* he knew how God would heal him, and when things didn't turn out like he thought, he was insulted! To be honest, *I* was a little insulted that God didn't perform in my box.

This is where the problem lies when we try to place God in a box. The moment He does something outside of our box, we view it as "unclean," just as Naaman thought God's method of healing in the river was unclean. But really, the only unclean thing is our lack of trust in God's plan.

Tijuana was my Jordan River. In my mind, it wasn't the best plan, but I went anyway, kicking and screaming. And to my surprise—like Naaman's—after God dunked me in Tijuana, I came back healed!

Outside of the Box

So many people who experience tragedy walk around with shame because things didn't turn out the way they expected. Maybe the marriage you fought and prayed for ended in divorce. Maybe the loved one for whom you prayed and believed in healing passed away. Maybe you had to take medication or seek other treatment for a season to get you through your illness. Maybe you had to see a counselor to help you make sense of it all. Maybe you succumbed to depression for a while.

The box is trying to shame you and tell you that you have failed—that you didn't have enough faith and God is disappointed in how you handled yourself in this season.

But it's not true! God loves you and has been with you every step of the way. Sometimes it takes more faith to leave your box than to stay. It requires more faith to go against the expectations of everyone around you in order to move toward healing.

I look back on my experiences now and think about how much easier (and cheaper) it would have been to receive an instantaneous miracle. But I can also see the tremendous value in the path down which God led me.

Every Last Crumb

I am reminded of the story of the fishes and loaves. After Jesus finished the miraculous feeding of the people, He instructed His disciples to collect all of the leftovers in baskets so nothing would be wasted (Matthew 14:13–21).

I love this story because it paints a beautiful picture of the God who doesn't waste anything. Every last piece, every last crumb, is worth saving to God. There is nothing He doesn't want to redeem! He wants to use every situation, circumstance, pain, doubt, disappointment, and victory to create something spectacular in our lives.

It's kind of like baking a cake. The individual ingredients by themselves might be too bitter, too sweet, or too salty, but when they are all mixed together and placed in the right environment for the right amount of time, something glorious is created!

I didn't necessarily like all the ingredients of my miracle, but I loved the outcome. Going to Mexico for treatment was far outside of my God-box at the time, but now I am grateful He led me down that road. It was there I learned that God didn't live in the box I had created for Him. To the contrary, His love, power, and ways are absolutely limitless!

Next, I will share with you just a few of the things I learned—lessons I wouldn't trade for the world—on my journey to Tijuana.

Tijuana Gave Me Courage

Courage means doing something in the face of pain or grief. Both pain and grief were my constant companions after I was diagnosed, and to make a move forward with those two by my side was the hardest thing I had ever done.

Anyone can make the right move when things are going well—when their health is good, the marriage is rocking along, and there is money in the bank. But continuing forward when some of those things aren't going so smoothly takes courage.

I used to hate fear, doubt and pain, but now I realize that without them, there is no reason for faith and courage. If nothing ever comes against us, then we don't ever know what it feels like to look doubt and fear in the face and continue on regardless.

There were many incidents along my journey to Tijuana, and while I was there, that required me to decide consciously to keep moving despite my pain and fear. One instance in particular comes to my mind.

As you can imagine, I was feeling pretty nervous about leaving my family for a month. Kissing my wife and kids goodbye at the airport and not knowing what to expect was almost more than I could take. I was a complete mess on the three-hour flight to San Diego.

After I landed, the sunny San Diego weather momentarily induced feelings of peace and calm as I stepped out of the airport. Yet these feelings slowly slipped away with each step closer to Tijuana.

A ragged blue van with a Rubio Cancer Center sticker pulled up, with a small Hispanic man driving. I reluctantly got in and we began our journey to the border. There wasn't a whole lot of talking, because we didn't speak the same language.

I was amazed at how easy it was to cross the border into Mexico. Tijuana wasn't a whole lot different than I imagined. I had been to Mexico many times on mission trips, and Tijuana was similar to the various cities I had visited there, only on a much larger scale.

About thirty minutes after we crossed the border, I asked the driver if we were close. He signaled that it was just around the corner.

To my surprise, we turned down a narrow street into what looked like a somewhat sketchy residential area. Knowing what the building looked like from pictures on the website, I began scanning for it. I was hoping this was just a shortcut to a more commercial district of the city.

Then the driver took a left turn onto a back alley that I could tell immediately was a dead end. It could have meant only one of two things: either he was going to cut out my kidney and leave me for dead, or this was where the clinic was located.

Thankfully, at the end of the alley, I recognized the building I had seen in the pictures. I experienced a brief moment of relief that my kidney was safe, but then began to panic that this was where my doctor was located. Surely there could be no legitimate answer for cancer down a back alley in Tijuana! If there was no answer from the best doctors in the best facilities in the United States, there could be no hope at the end of this alley.

I completely freaked out. I yelled one of the three Spanish words I knew: *"Alto!"* ("Stop!"). The driver halted the car.

In that moment, I felt more alone and afraid than I ever had before in my life. Everything in me wanted to go back home. But instead, I reached down deep into a place of faith that I had no clue even existed and motioned to the diver to continue.

Fleeting as it was and minor as it may seem, that moment in that alley marks one of my greatest acts of courage. I was outside of my box in uncharted waters. I was scared, alone, and hurting. Yet I kept moving forward—toward healing.

In that moment I had nothing but my faith in God's plan for my life. Then it felt like certain death, but now it feels like life and victory! I am forever grateful for that alley tucked away in Tijuana, Mexico, and for the courage it gave me.

Tijuana Gave Me Trust in God's Financial Supply

Rachel and I have been tithers and givers since before we were married. God has supplied our every need along the way, but our needs were never especially great. It wasn't until our decision for me to go to Tijuana that I really had to trust God as our financial supplier.

The cost for the first month of treatment was going to be $26,000. That amount was just shy of what I earned in a year from my position at our church. It might as well have been a million dollars! We had no savings or any other way of paying for it. Our respective parents at the time were in difficult times financially and didn't have a lot of cash to offer us, either.

I remember calling my mom, crying in discouragement and saying, "Mom, I just don't know how this is going to happen."

I will never forget her response: "Kolbe, either God will supply the money or you won't get to go."

Her words represented a bit too much stark reality for my comfort, but she was right. If God didn't provide a miracle financially, I couldn't get the treatment.

Then she continued, "But $26,000 is nothing to a God who has everything!" I agreed with her and was somewhat encouraged, but the reality of the situation still weighed heavily on me.

About ten minutes after I got off the phone, she called me back. I answered, and this time she was crying. However, I could tell her tears weren't tears of sadness, but of joy. She informed me that she had just gotten off the phone with a friend of the family who had already put a check in the mail for $13,000!

I couldn't believe it. We cried together as she declared through her tears, "God is going to do this!" After that, my faith was strong that God absolutely would supply our every need.

A few days later, I went to the mailbox and found a check for $4,000 from a Presbyterian church in a neighboring town. I had never been Presbyterian! In fact, I didn't even know many Presbyterians. But they had heard about my situation and decided to help me out. Hallelujah! Thank God for that little Presbyterian church!

I could tell story after story about miracle gifts we received that made it possible for me to seek treatment in Mexico. Over the course of the last six years, Rachel and I have paid many more thousands of dollars for treatment, plane tickets, and related expenses, and have not a penny of debt to show for it. There is no way of explaining this without echoing the words of my mother: "God did it!"

Had we not faced a tremendous financial need, we would have never experienced God's tremendous supply. This revelation of God's providence was truly priceless!

Tijuana Gave Me My Playlist

Many of us have music playlists on our smartphones or other devices for just about every different type of moment we can think of. We have a playlist for working out, for throwing a party, or for simply listening to music at work. Nothing helps get you through a workout session or a long day at work like the right soundtrack!

These are songs that fit and complement the mood of what you are trying to accomplish. You don't listen to sweet worship music when you are exercising—you listen to the *Rocky* theme. Instead of listening to sad songs when you are throwing a party, you put on some dance music. You don't listen to that country song about getting a divorce when you are alone with your lady—you throw on some Marvin Gaye! But what about a playlist for the difficult times?

After about two days of being in the Mexican clinic, I was a mess. Physically, my body was uncomfortable from the treatment. Mentally, I was depressed, and spiritually I was feeling lost.

As I sat alone in my little room—bored out of my mind, 1,500 miles from my family and feeling even farther from God—I got my phone out. Since I had no service in Mexico, social media and nearly every other app I had on my phone were not options. So I decided to open my downloaded music.

I hit "Play" and the song "Worth It All" by Rita Springer began. In three and a half minutes, I went from depressed and far from God to crying and worshiping in His presence.

That's when I came up with my plan to make my tragedy playlist. This playlist included songs that invited the presence of God while creating a mood of faith and an atmosphere of hope! I would sit in my room, hooked up to IVs, with my playlist running while I worshiped God as I never had before.

These songs were no longer just songs, but weapons with which to fight! When I felt alone, I played songs about God's presence. When I felt betrayed by Him, I played songs about His faithfulness. When I felt hopeless, I played songs full of hope. When I felt like quitting, I played songs about not giving up. When I felt discouraged, I played songs about God working out all things for the good. When I was thinking about myself, I would sing along with songs focused on Him. When I felt like my life might be over, I would sing along with songs about my future.

Thus, in that tiny little room in Tijuana Mexico, I grew closer to God than I had ever been before. This happened because I had the courage to make a simple playlist and worship God with all my heart!

Here are a few of the songs on my list. They might be a bit dated now, but they helped me through the darkest time in my life:

- "Bring It All Together" (Natalie Grant, featuring Wynonna Judd)
- "If Not for Your Grace" (Israel and New Breed)
- "My Hope" (Darlene Zschech)
- "Worth It All" (Rita Springer)
- "Can't Give Up Now" (Mary Mary)
- "Moving Forward (Israel and New Breed)
- "Day after Day" (Kristian Stanfill)
- "Use Me" (Ron Kenoly)
- "Alpha and Omega" (Israel and New Breed)
- "Follow You" (Leeland)

I don't know what kind of music you listen to, but I encourage you to create a playlist that fosters an atmosphere of hope and a mood of faith. Play it loud and begin to worship your great big God!

Tijuana Gave Me Olga

My treatment in Mexico went beyond traditional treatment of chemo and radiation—it included natural therapies as well. The one I was least excited about was enemas.

That's right. Enemas.

To make matters worse, on my second day at the clinic, I was instructed to go see "Olga" to receive my first enema. I was a little panicked because I wasn't sure beforehand whether Olga was a dude or a lady.

Much to my relief, Olga was a sweet Hispanic lady. I wasn't sure what to say to her. "Hi, I'm here for my enema?" Should I shake her hand? Do I just pull down my pants? I mean, what was the protocol here? It was awkward, to say the least.

To my surprise she told me (in English) to sit down, and she put on a pot of coffee. I thought, "Okay, we're going to get to know each other before we do this." But the coffee wasn't for us to drink. All I could think was, "She better let that stuff cool off first!"

The initial session was difficult, but after losing every ounce of pride and manhood I had, I endured.

Over the next few weeks, in fact, I began to look forward to my visits to Olga. I simply regarded it as I would a trip to Starbucks—in a way. Moreover, she was one of the few people there who spoke English. I knew severe loneliness was setting in when I looked forward to my visits with the Spanish lady who gave me enemas.

During our conversations, I found out that Olga was a strong believer in Jesus and a faithful churchgoer. She was fascinated by the fact I was a pastor and loved to ask me questions about the faith.

Of all the topics we discussed, she had the most questions about the baptism of the Holy Spirit. She told me she went to a church that believed in it, but she had never received it personally. I encouraged her to pray and speak to her pastor on the subject.

Olga's church stood only a few blocks from the clinic, so she invited me to attend. I wasn't sure I wanted to brave the streets of Tijuana on foot, but she kept asking and I finally relented. I hadn't packed church clothes, so I put on a hoodie and some sweatpants and headed out.

I knew I was headed in the right direction because I could hear the music playing from two blocks away. The two-story church building, with its painted white exterior and tiled interior, instantly stood out from the surrounding shacks—and its pews were packed with hundreds of people praising God.

The Spirit of God was present and I immediately felt right at home. Even though I didn't have a clue what they were saying, I enjoyed the sermon—I simply shouted out "Gloria Dios" every few minutes in an effort to fit in!

When it came time for the altar call, many people went to the front for prayer. Others began to pray for each other in their seats. It was a powerful moment in the service. I was just sitting with my eyes closed and thanking God for His presence when I felt a tap on my shoulder.

It was Olga. Her eyes were filled with tears as she asked if she could pray for me. Of course, I said yes and welcomed her prayer. After she finished praying, she asked if I would pray for her to receive the baptism of the Holy Spirit. I was thrilled—but before I even began my prayer, she burst out into her prayer language! It was beautiful.

For a moment I forgot where I was and why I was there. All that mattered was that this lady had decided to take a step of faith with her Savior. Even in the midst of the greatest difficulty of my life, God still wanted to use me to reach out to others with His love!

It has now been over six years since I have seen Olga, but I would like to think she remembers me the same way I remember her: as someone who deeply impacted her life with the love of Jesus.

I encourage you, even in your most difficult hour, to keep an eye out for *your* Olga. You never know when someone who needs encouragement will cross your path. The experience might just encourage you most of all. Don't miss it!

Trusting God Where You Are

In the story of Naaman, there wasn't anything special about the Jordan River. Rather, there was something special about trusting God. In my case, I don't think it was Tijuana that was so special, but the experience of trusting God in the midst of being there. Wherever you are, learn to trust Him!

If everything hasn't turned out the way you thought it would or should, don't let shame and disappointment fill your heart. God is not limited in any way, shape, or form in how He can move in your life. Tijuana felt like God's wrath when I was there, but now I can see it as God's grace and goodness.

The enemy wants doubt and depression to overtake you in this season, but I encourage you to keep trusting God. He is not limited to the box you have created for Him. To the contrary, He is with you every step you take! Stop now and declare that good things are coming out of this season in your life—whether you can see them now or not.

Chapter 9 Questions

Question: In what box, or set of expectations, have you tried to restrict God in your mind and your heart? How or why did you create this box? How has God provided for you outside of this box—that is, in spite of your expectations?

_____

_____

_____

_____

_____

_____

_____

_____

_____

_____

_____

Question: How, specifically, can you grow in listening to God, rather than your or others' expectations, for direction? To which people in your life might He be leading you to receive or give encouragement?

_____

_____

_____

_____

_____

_____

_____

_____

_____

_____

_____

_____

Action: Don't try to keep God in a box of your or others' expectations. Instead, have the courage to listen to God Himself, and His Word, for direction. Find courage in His supply and providence, and look for opportunities to find and give encouragement to others whom God puts your path.

Chapter 9 Notes

A Step Toward the Light

Are you fighting with God's tools, but without *Him*? If so, it's time for you to run to God and allow Him to take up your fight for you. I can assure you from experience that the latter is much better.

If this is where you are, don't feel ashamed. I was right there with you. I didn't stay there though, and neither should you. Get alone with your heavenly Father and let Him minister to you. It will be a supernatural work only He can do. Let God fill you with His life as you begin to trust Him one day at a time.

As you do, there is no doubt He will take that tomb stone and turn it into a stepping stone. He will take that prison and turn it into a pulpit. He will take that tragedy and turn it into triumph.

At the time of writing this conclusion, it has been six years since I received the phone call telling me I had cancer. It's been six years since I was given six months to live. As I mentioned in the first chapter, my family and my church prayed hard for a miracle, and at times we were frustrated when our miracle did not manifest the way we thought it should—which was immediately. I can see now that God *was* working a miracle in my life, but it was in His timing.

I now have the testimony to share that for the past five years I have been completely and totally cancer free, a miracle to be sure. It wasn't the "touch and—poof—you are healed" kind of miracle. Instead, it was the "trust and walk it out" kind of miracle.

Most of the pages you have just read were written during the early days of my diagnosis. They are the practical spiritual principles I learned and applied as I stood in faith during my life's darkest hours.

Now don't get me wrong—I was not always graceful in applying these truths. When I was a kid, my dad always told me I was like a bull in a China shop—knocking things over and causing chaos with every step I took. If you had a front row seat to my miracle, I imagine that "bull in a china shop" is probably what I looked like most of the time. I struggled and fumbled around. I doubted and got angry. I blamed and had a bad attitude.

Through all of these things, however, my heavenly Father never left me, and I never left Him. I am so glad God was not grading me on my performance through the tragedy, because I would have failed miserably.

Jesus had already passed every test. All I had to do was trust in the finished work of the cross, and allow Him to live that out in and through me.

My miracle reminds me of the artists who paint during worship on stage at a church or summer camp. They sling paint onto a giant canvas and wipe it all around as if there is no rhyme or reason to what they are doing. It looks like a huge mess, and from the audience you are wondering if this person has ever painted before. Then at the last moment, when the audience's doubt is at its highest, the artist turns the painting upside down and *boom!* What looked like a complete mess turns out to be a masterpiece painting.

That is the best way I can describe my healing. Most of the time, I wondered if this was God's first time dealing with a tragic situation. I couldn't understand what He was doing. But then He turned my life upside down, and now everyone can see it—I am healed. *Hallelujah!*

Had it not been for the revelations now recorded in these pages, I have no doubt I would not be here today. For me, each chapter represents a step toward life and healing, but ultimately, toward Him. They represent a step toward the light of Christ in the midst of the darkness of tragedy.

I know what these truths mean for me. My prayer is that as the Lord makes them real in your life, you would likewise begin to move toward the Light.

I know you may not feel like it now, but I can assure you that if you stay in Christ, your best days are ahead. You, too, can be triumphant in tragedy!

Notes

1. Zschech, Darlene. "My Hope." *Hope*. Hillsong Music Australia, 2003.
2. "The Books of the Bible." *Blue Letter Bible*. https://www.blueletterbible.org/study/misc/66boo ks.cfm
3. Sermon Central Staff. "Boy and Baseball Bat." *Sermon Central*. 18 June 2007. https://www.sermoncentral.com/illustrations/ser mon-illustration-sermoncentral-staff-stories-god-brings-purpose-61505
4. Wilcox, Peter C. *There Are No Right Answers to Wrong Questions. 15 Ways Our Questions Influence Our Choices to Live a Christian Life.* Resource Publications, 2016.
5. "The Names of God in the Old Testament." *Blue Letter Bible*. https://www.blueletterbible.org/study/misc/name_god.cfm
6. Cole, Steven J. "Lesson 34: The God Who Sees (Genesis 16:7–16)." *Bible.org.* 1996.

https://bible.org/seriespage/lesson-34-god-who-sees-genesis-167-16

7. Wanjek, Christopher. "Media Too Optimistic about Cancer, Scientists Say." 16 March 2010. *Live Science*. http://www.livescience.com/10963-media-optimistic-cancer-scientists.html

8. "Strong's G859 – Aphesis." *Blue Letter Bible*. https://www.blueletterbible.org/lang/lexicon/lexicon.cfm?Strongs=G859&t=KJV

9. "Covet." *The Free Dictionary*. Farlex, Inc. http://www.thefreedictionary.com/covet

About the Author

Kolbe Hill is the associate pastor of The Remnant Church, a thriving congregation in the small town of La Grange, Texas. He is a passionate communicator of God's Word, bringing hope, encouragement, and laughter to everyone to whom he ministers. Aside from preaching, Kolbe's passions include shopping (per his wife), enjoying the outdoors, and spending time with his family. Kolbe and his wife Rachel have been married since 2003 and have two beautiful daughters.

Made in the USA
Columbia, SC
22 February 2020

88124215R00093